# Endorsements

"This book is an outstanding compilation of stories from such a diverse group of women, all of whom experienced similar grief, yet assurance in their beliefs. Anyone who has suffered the loss of a mother or a mother figure should read this book. It is a great connection to the fact that suffering is real, but there always remains hope."

**Jody Correa**
Hospice Volunteer Coordinator

"With deep sensitivity born of the loss of her own mother when she was seven, Myrna Folkert has lovingly written a book for all who have lost their own mothers at any age. They say books can be both mirrors and windows--mirrors showing us more clearly our own reality and windows teaching us about other people and their experiences. This book is mostly a mirror for those who still ache from that most crucial of losses-- the loss of a mother. Readers will gain clarity, compassion, and understanding for their own grief, no matter how long it has been since their mothers died. Beginning with her own heartbreaking story and expanding into the stories of others, Myrna Folkert takes the reader gently by the hand on a journey of mourning and healing, loss and hope."

**Lorilee Craker**
Author of *Anne of Green Gables, My Daughter and Me: What My Favorite Book Taught Me About Grace, Belonging and the Orphan in Us All*; *Money Secrets of the Amish*, *Through the Storm* with Lynne Spears & *My Journey to Heaven* with Marv Besteman

"I'm thankful for the vulnerability and transparency of the women who have shared their stories of deep loss and sure hope, found in their faith. I discovered helpful ideas for grieving and was encouraged as I personally related to the thoughts and feelings of those who have walked this same road before me. What a great resource!"

**Rev. Gina Dick**
Pastor, teacher, registered nurse, fellow daughter of hope

"Daughters of Hope offers soul-stirring stories and comforting words of encouragement and warmth. This book answers the hearts crying out in grief and promotes healing, grace, and understanding. Myrna Folkert highlights God's wisdom throughout, and in perfect measure. A fantastic book for individuals or small groups."

**Kim de Blecourt**
Author of *Until We All Come Home* and *I Call You Mine*

"Having recently lost my mother, I thought this book would be hard to read, but it was just what I needed. Even though my mom was in her 90's, losing a mother is a life-altering experience that is difficult to navigate. Thanks to the brave daughters who openly share their stories, we have a support group who can walk beside us on our journey of grief. I especially love how the women recall the simple moments of cooking and baking with their mothers— moments I can relate to, and memories that will last a lifetime. Lessons of faith are peppered throughout the stories, and the Bible verses are inspiring and filled with comfort and hope."

**Crystal Bowman**
Award-winning author of more than 100 books for women and children, including, *Our Daily Bread for Kids*, and *Mothers in Waiting*

"In *Daughters of Hope: Thriving after Mother Loss,* Myrna Folkert has produced an excellent resource for anyone who has lost a mother. She has recorded the touching story-interviews of women of faith who have suffered such a loss. Helpful Biblical advice is woven into their testimonies. Her personal account of losing her devout mother at the tender age of seven, brought tears to my own eyes. As a Christian psychiatrist, I am aware that many people fail to fully grieve these losses. Depression, anxieties, and delayed grief reactions may occur. This volume should become a welcome source of comfort and healing to many grieving people of faith."

**Robert W. Miner, MD**

"As someone shaped by the loss of her mother at a young age, Myrna Folkert writes with sensitivity and compassion, offering hope to daughters who grieve and pointing to the trustworthy presence of the God who weeps with us. I'm grateful for the courage of the women who shared through interviews their experiences of bereavement. Those who are navigating their own loss of a mother will find comfort, encouragement, and solidarity in these stories."

**Sharon Garlough Brown**
Author of the *Sensible Shoes* series and *Shades of Light*

"Powerful! This book will pull you in from the beginning. A compilation of stories as well as emotions. A reminder of the importance to fully engage in your own life, grieve your losses and remember to celebrate life along your journey."

**Susan Hofland, MA, LLPC**

# DAUGHTERS OF HOPE

## Thriving after Mother Loss

### Myrna Folkert

Copyright © Myrna Folkert, 2020

All rights reserved. No part of this publication may be reproduced or transmitted in any form or by any electronic or mechanical means including photo copying, recording, or any information storage and retrieval system now known or to be invented, without permission in writing from the author.

All Scripture quotations, unless otherwise indicated, are from The Holy Bible, New International Version®, NIV® Copyright © 1973, 1978, 1984, 2011 by Biblica, Inc.™ Used by permission. All rights reserved worldwide.

Scripture quotation marked (NASB) are taken from the NEW AMERICAN STANDARD BIBLE, Copyright © 1960, 1962, 1963, 1968, 1971, 1972, 1973, 1975, 1977 by the Lockman Foundation. Used by permission.

Scriptures marked (NLT) are taken from the Holy Bible, New Living Translation, copyright © 1996, 2004, 2007, 2013, 2015 by Tyndale House Foundation. Used by permission of Tyndale House Publishers, Inc., Carol Stream, Illinois 60188. All rights reserved.

Scripture quotations marked with ESV, are from the ESV® Bible (The Holy Bible, English Standard Version®), copyright © 2001 by Crossway, a publishing ministry of Good News Publishers. Used by permission. All rights reserved.

Scriptures marked GNB are taken from the GOOD NEWS BIBLE (GNB): Scriptures taken from the Good News Bible © 1994 published by the Bible Societies/HarperCollins Publishers Ltd UK, Good News Bible© American Bible Society 1966, 1971, 1976, 1992. Used with permission.

Scripture marked NKJV taken from the New King James Version. Copyright © 1982 by Thomas Nelson, Inc. Used by permission. All rights reserved.

Scriptures marked KJV are taken from the KING JAMES VERSION: a public domain in the United States.

The events and conversations in this book have been set down to the best of the author's ability, although some names and details have been altered to protect the privacy of individuals.

Quote by Dann Stouten used by permission.

Photos were submitted by the participants, with full permission for use.

First paperback edition February 2020

Name: Folkert, Myrna    www.myrnafolkert.com

Title: Daughters of Hope: Thriving after Mother Loss

Identifiers:

LCCN: 2020901855

ISBN: 978-0-578-64093-8

Subjects: 1. Family & Relationships—Death, Grief, Bereavement

2. Religion—Christian Life—Women's Issues

## *Dedication*

Written in honor of my mom,
Martha Kleinheksel,
who is playing
piano, bass, accordion, and guitar
in heaven!
I'm thankful for your spiritual influence on me.
I can't wait to see you again.

# Gratitude

To Word Weavers writing group of Holland/Zeeland, MI., and my online group, called, *Page 18*. Your encouragement, prayers, critique, and ideas helped me immensely.

For Christian writing conferences that provided loads of information and many new friends: Maranatha Christian Writers' Conference, Breathe Christian Writers' Conference, The Well, and Carol Kent's Speak Up Conference.

Thank you to my dear sweet aunts, Pauline Volkema and Lois Blanchard. The emails, prayers, notes, and comments urged me to keep writing.

To my sisters, Eloise Shattuck and Cindy Kleinheksel, you've been there my whole life. You went through it too from a different perspective; our hearts are forever connected as only sisters can be.

To lifetime friends, Shellie Scholten, Jane Klingenberg, and Luann Mullen, I couldn't have made it without your prayers and encouragement along the way. You knew me then; you know me now. I'm thankful for you.

Heartfelt gratitude to my beta readers—Bonnie Sue Beardsley, Kathy Bruins, and Beth Crosby, and my editors and proofreaders, Denise Vredevoogd, Carol Graft, Beth Foreman, Jan Afman, Pat Sabin, and Laurel Ralya. Your gift of time is so appreciated.

In honor of my beloved Ruth VanHeukelom, your friendship and prayers were beyond a treasure, our long talks precious. You're sorely missed. Looking forward to sitting with you again in heaven.

To my cherished friend, Ruth Trippy, you were an angel sent to help me through some dark times. Your spiritual and writing mentorship is priceless to me. My heart is full with thankfulness.

To Cliff, my patient, solid rock husband, who supported my writing by making the way for me to attend writing conferences, giving tech support, and always loving me well. I love you.

Most of all, praise to God who sustains and holds me. He's been faithful throughout my life and I thank Him. All glory goes to Him for anything I've accomplished.

# Introduction

Many women have questions when their mothers pass away, like "Why?" or "How am I going to live without her?" Even those who lost their mother years ago may still ponder these kinds of questions. Many daughters must deal with the pain without support. Thus, *Daughters of Hope: Thriving after Mother Loss,* presents stories of mother-loss and the prevailing hope the daughters have because of their faith in God.

I lost my mother unexpectedly when I was seven years old. Later, even as a teenager, I felt led by God to write a book about the loss, knowing there had to be a purpose for the tragedy. With the Lord's hand upholding me, I abided in Him throughout my life. He has always proved Himself faithful and never let me go. The time has finally come for me to share about my mother-loss.

While researching this subject, I discovered a national survey by Comfort Zone Camps, that showed 11 percent (one in nine) of people in our nation experience the death of a parent by the age of twenty. Various blog and newspaper articles pertaining to mother-loss are listed in the resources section in the back of the book. Comparable books on this topic didn't produce an adequate text from the perspective of Christian women whose mothers have died. Many interviewed women read books on grief or even mother-loss but found none based on Christians' experiences. These statistics and articles amazed me but piqued my desire to help those suffering this devastating time in their lives.

Over the last few years, I've interviewed twenty-seven brave women willing to come to the microphone believing their story might offer hope to others. Laughter and tears spilled during these sacred conversations. I interviewed them about what happened and how the Lord moved in their situations. Later, I transcribed and revised each woman's recorded interview into story form.

Most of the interviewees were surprised at themselves and apologized with the claim they hadn't cried this much about their mothers for many years. It's my belief that getting their story out assisted in healing and cleansing their hearts. Talking about their mothers proved to be a precious time of remembrance. Even in cases of strained relationships, a mother-daughter bond remained. As I was allowed into these women's deep personal thoughts and recollections, I dipped further into memories of my mother's death.

One of the most poignant comments I received during the interviews, was, "How often do you get to talk about your mother for two hours straight, and someone just listens?" Many others expressed it was like therapy to talk about one of the most important people they ever had in their lives—their mother.

The participants were women of different ages, walks, and seasons of life. Some were mothers, while others did not have children of their own. Some had strong relationships with their mothers and others did not.

The cause of the mothers' deaths varied. Several women managed to survive the agony of witnessing a long slow death, like Judy D., whose mother had Alzheimer's disease for fourteen years. Others suffered a complete shock, like Ruthann, who flew home from missionary work in Africa when her mother suddenly died in a plane crash.

All the women I interviewed for this book had faith in the Lord at the time of their mother's death. They shared their emotions and actions at various stages during their mothers' illnesses and how each one is coping after her death. They commonly noted they missed their mom the most at major life transitions—such as their weddings and the birth of children. Since many women offered these answers, these areas were not usually expounded upon in their individual accounts. The unique parts are shared in detail.

The loss of a mother will always be difficult no matter the age of the mother or daughter. For the daughter, it requires a lifelong process of adapting. Whether your mother died one month or many years ago, it still happened.

I'm praying you will be blessed and encouraged as you read their precious accounts. May you realize you're not alone; others have experienced similar trials. You are in a forum of kindred spirits. We can pass one another a tissue and offer a hand of assistance.

The ladies testified that the Lord is faithful, His ways are perfect, and His ways are much higher than our ways. We sometimes don't like His ways, but His character—who God is—remains the same. He is God, He is present, and He loves us.

If you are a believer in God, you will relate to the faith expressed by these women. If you are not a believer, please listen to hear how they put one foot in front of the other and depended on God to help them through.

Discussion questions are included for book clubs or grief groups. Counselors, pastors, and people who live with or around bereaved daughters may obtain assistance through this book and the resources offered. They will want to recommend it to their clients, loved ones, or friends. Included are ideas for honoring and celebrating mothers, or to help in the mother-loss grief process. It is my prayer that it will comfort any person who has lost a loved one, not only a daughter whose mother has died.

Emotions may well up while you read, but you will see hope expressed throughout the book. I pray you gain strength from these stories, find a way to move forward in life, keeping memories of your mother alive.

Each interviewee made it clear they miss their loved one and grieve, but in a different way. They have hope that comes from knowing Jesus Christ and the assurance of His death and resurrection which secured salvation for believers. This book points to God's promises of comfort, peace and eternity with Him as the true source of hope in facing grief. As Christ followers, we believe we will be with Him in heaven when we die, and we'll greet our fellow believers there.

God can put a soothing balm of comfort on your heart when you're grieving. He provides the Holy Spirit, His holy words in the Bible, and other people to help us through life's sorrows. May God's promises uplift you and the power of the Holy Spirit permeate every fiber of your soul with hope.

# CONTENTS

| | | |
|---|---|---|
| | Endorsements | i |
| | Gratitude | vi |
| | Introduction | viii |
| **Author's Story** | | 1 |
| Chapter 1 | A Rude Awakening | 2 |
| Chapter 2 | The Swing | 5 |
| Chapter 3 | Casseroles, Anger, and Bargaining | 8 |
| Chapter 4 | Words of Love | 12 |
| Chapter 5 | Searching and Finding | 15 |
| Chapter 6 | What Will Happen to Me? | 17 |
| Chapter 7 | Patent Leather Traditions | 19 |
| Chapter 8 | Delayed Grief | 21 |
| Chapter 9 | Our God of Hope | 23 |
| **Other Women's Stories** | | 30 |
| **Younger than Twenty when Mom Died** | | 31 |
| Chapter 10 | Marie Getz - Journaling was a Friend | 32 |
| Chapter 11 | Mary Sterenberg - Mama Ran her Fingers Through my Hair | 38 |
| Chapter 12 | Rebecca Deng - Escape from Sudan | 45 |
| **Two Sisters Got Through It Together** | | 50 |
| Chapter 13 | Carla - One Little Rose | 51 |
| Chapter 14 | Lisa - Star Gazing | 58 |
| **Four Sisters, Two Moms' Deaths** | | 65 |
| Chapter 15 | Marilyn Tinklenberg - Meet Me Over in Glory Land | 66 |
| Chapter 16 | Carol Teske - Held by the Everlasting Arms | 70 |
| Chapter 17 | Nancy Maas - Pass the Blessing On | 74 |
| Chapter 18 | Faith VanArendonk - Longing to See | 80 |

| | | |
|---|---|---|
| **In Their Twenties When Mom Died** | | 85 |
| Chapter 19 | Kari - Bitter or Better | 86 |
| Chapter 20 | Elaine Stock - A Challenging Childhood | 92 |
| Chapter 21 | Karen Blakley - Spending Quality Time | 98 |
| Chapter 22 | Rachael Smith - Light Shines Brightest in the Dark | 103 |
| Chapter 23 | Vanessa Jorge - Caught Up Together in the Clouds | 109 |
| Chapter 24 | Ruthann David - I Plan to Give You a Hope and a Future | 116 |
| Chapter 25 | Judy Boeve - Nothing Can Separate Us | 122 |
| **In Their Thirties When Mom Died** | | 130 |
| Chapter 26 | Rachel Brink - I'm Going to See Jesus | 131 |
| Chapter 27 | Janice Broyles - Run to God | 138 |
| Chapter 28 | Michele Dekker - Wipe Every Tear | 142 |
| Chapter 29 | Joy Meyer - Without Faith, It Would Be Hopeless | 149 |
| Chapter 30 | Pat Lubben - I'll Hold Your Right Hand | 154 |
| Chapter 31 | Julie Peters - The Peace of Knowing | 160 |
| Chapter 32 | Jodi Vande Noord - It's Time for Me to Go | 166 |
| **In Their Fifties When Mom Died** | | 173 |
| Chapter 33 | Prudy Berghorst - Be Available | 174 |
| Chapter 34 | Marcia - This is the Day that the Lord Has Made | 180 |
| Chapter 35 | Hope Doolaard - Deeper Than a Best Friend | 186 |
| Chapter 36 | Judy Dunagan - A Very Long Goodbye | 193 |

## Resources                                                                 198

| | |
|---|---|
| Healing Balm for The Soul | 198 |
| Bible Verses to Comfort and Encourage | 200 |
| Support and Helps | 202 |
| Sources/Research of Motherless Daughters | 204 |
| Discussion Questions | 205 |
| Get to Know the Daughters | 207 |
| Author Biography | 219 |

# THE AUTHOR'S STORY

# Chapter 1

# A Rude Awakening

*So that you do not grieve like the rest of mankind, who have no hope.*
1 Thessalonians 4:13

"You have to get up and get dressed. Mommy died in her sleep," Eloise said.

A skinny seven-year-old, not fully awake, I felt like a rag doll tossed hurriedly around. Standing next to my bed in the morning coolness, I was hearing but not yet comprehending.

My oldest sister Eloise and my sister-in-law Sherry woke me. What were they saying as they swooped up my nightie and grabbed a nearby shirt to pull over my head? Why would Sherry be in our house so early on . . . Ahh . . . is it Sunday morning? She lived next door, but the grayness of night still hung dim in the huge farmhouse. Even though my east window shade was pulled down, I knew this was an unusual hour.

The phone was ringing. People mumbled and moved around. No pans clanked. No bacon sizzled. The normal breakfast smells were absent. No friendly voices talked about the chickens and what chores were accomplished out in the farmyard. When I was dressed, Eloise led me by the hand into the living room just a few steps from my bedroom.

While I rubbed the sleep out of my eyes, I was set between my other two sisters on the davenport. The youngest of six children, I was used to being placed in small spaces or on people's laps.

My two older brothers were in the house, dressed in their work clothes, and stood in the double doorway to the dining room. Sherry joined my brother, John, her husband of only six months, on the left, while Ron, the oldest, leaned against the opposite side of the doorframe.

My daddy held the front door open for two strange men in black suits to enter the house. They exchanged polite hellos and spoke in hushed tones with him near my parents' closed bedroom. On my right, my sister Audrey's mouth hung half-open, and tears ran down her pale face. The suited men discussed with my daddy something about . . . how to bring her outside? *Just let my mommy sleep a little longer, and she will wake up and make us all breakfast with a smile like she always does.*

After they stepped outside for a moment, the two suited men returned carrying a long board with white sheets on it. They entered my parents' bedroom with my daddy, and shut the door deliberately. I heard it latch with a click. Loud bumping and rumbling noises came from behind the door. My brothers and sisters shifted uncomfortably or cleared their throats.

I figured this must be a very serious situation because of how all my older siblings acted. I had heard the word death before, but it was something that happened to other people or very old people. With my tiny hands, I grabbed the knee of my sister Cindy on one side, and Audrey's on the other. My heart beat fast. I wondered why the men made so much noise in there.

Finally, the bedroom door opened. A burning sensation crawled up inside my body from my toes to my head. I covered my mouth with my hand.

The suited men stood on each end of the bed-like board. With a quick upward snap of their wrists, they caused wheels to lower with a loud clink and lock. The bed with zigzag legs carried the form of a body under the sheets, neatly tucked in on all sides. Even the head was concealed with careful folding at the top. I supposed my mommy was under there. I wondered how she could breathe that way. *Surely, the hospital would make her well again.*

My daddy's face was as white as the sheets as he trudged behind them. He stopped at the threshold of the front door to watch.

Turning my body around, I wedged my knees between my sisters and grabbed the back of the davenport to see where my mommy was going. Barely daring to pull back the sheer curtain on the large farmhouse window, I watched the men slide the board into the back of a long black car. They slammed the back doors, got into their seats, and drove away.

With both hands, my daddy leaned his weight against the front door as he closed it, dragging hope out of the room like an airtight seal. He turned the skeleton key and paused in silence.

# Chapter 2

# The Swing

*You keep track of all my sorrows. You have collected all my tears in your bottle. You have recorded each one in your book.*
Psalm 56:8 NLT

When the big black car pulled away, my daddy did an about-face, walked through the dining room and kitchen, out the back of the house. The screen door slammed and bounced as he descended the steps and turned toward the barn. My brothers followed silently with lowered heads. My oldest sisters drifted to the kitchen table in tearful conversation.

I stretched out on the davenport, clasped my hands behind my head, and crossed one ankle over the other. It occurred to me that Audrey also slipped away. Being only three years apart, we usually shared everything. I wondered where she went.

After a few moments, my daddy reentered the house through the screen door in the kitchen and went into the dining room where the black telephone hung on the wall. He spread the phone book out on the nearby ironing board and placed calls to relatives and friends. My daddy's unemotional repetition on the phone reminded me of a skipping LP on Eloise's record player as he relayed the information over and over that Martha died in her sleep during the night.

I believed my mommy must be dead after I listened to him say it so many times. I heard about the death of a grandma before, and I saw lifeless chickens or pigs on the farm. *But what was dead? Where was dead?*

My daddy's forefinger kept the phone dial winding back and forth, back and forth in a circular motion with a grinding cry.

Julia, one of my mommy's best friends, who lived across the street, came and sat in the kitchen with my sisters. They talked quietly to one another as they wiped their eyes and noses with tissues. I slipped past all of them and out the back door, unnoticed. My whereabouts were usually not of much concern in such a large and busy farm family.

The sun sparkled, and the air was unusually warm for a mid-March day in Michigan. I went to my swing, which hung from the middle tree on the west side of the house—a familiar spot. Audrey had often twirled baton nearby, we pushed each other in the swing, or I played there alone.

Sometimes my little game was planned—I timed it when my daddy was getting his overalls on preparing to do his chores. I'd swish past him to sit on the wooden board of the swing before he exited the back door. If I hit it just right, my daddy would notice me as he stepped down the pitted concrete steps.

I gave him my youngest girl-child look, and called out, "Daddy, will you give me a push?"

He chuckled as he deviated from his direct path to the barn, to stand behind me.

"Okay, so you want a push? Get ready!"

Daddy delivered a few delightful big-man pushes. I asked for more, but then he continued on to his farm work. The pushing wasn't so hard that it scared me but provided enough momentum so I could maintain a high speed for a long time if I pumped with my body. Those swing pushes were one of the few times my busy farmer daddy played with me.

I reveled in the breeze, letting my hair trail behind me as I leaned back while going forward, stretching my legs as far as I could. As soon as I reached the top of the crest, the swing would fall back. I curled my legs in, and the wind blew my blonde locks all around my face. Lean back, stretch out, curl legs, lean forward in a rhythm.

When the swinging dwindled down, I rolled onto the grass as a few of my beloved cats strolled over. They curiously drew near whenever I was outside. Calico with white boots, black, and tiger-colored ones rubbed past one of my legs, and then the other, while they curled their tails and raised their noses. I loved to smooth their silky backs, scratch their tummies and behind their ears, until they'd relax their bodies and pull in their claws. I scooched up against the side porch of the house and loaded as many kitties as I could on my lap. The purring was a dreamy melody as I gazed out over the cornfields at the western sky.

This morning was different. I wasn't in the swing to play, enjoy my cats, or to try to gain my daddy's attention. I sat in the motionless swing feeling numb. My mouth tasted like a dried-up piece of bread as I tried to make any sense of the morning's events. *Why was the sun shining brightly? Why were the birds singing cheerfully? Why were people rushing down the country road? Didn't they know what happened here?*

As I sat in the swing this time, I pushed myself slightly forward and backward with a toe that barely touched the ground. I heard a slight creaking noise above me. The rope emitted a straw-like smell and tiny particles of dust glittered in pillars of sunlight as they slowly circulated to the ground. *God, why did you take my mommy away from me?* I questioned. *Is she up there in heaven with you somewhere in the clouds?* I searched the sky for some answers. *She just hugged me last night after I said my prayers.* I remembered how we giggled as she returned the words, "I love you." I could still feel the kiss on my cheek and the scent of her hair whisper past.

As I hung on the right rope with both hands and pressed my wet face into my sleeve, I wondered how I would live without her.

Fear placed its ugly hands around my neck.

# Chapter 3

# Casseroles, Anger, and Bargaining

*Hear me, LORD, my plea is just; listen to my cry. Hear my prayer.*
Psalm 17:1

No one made eye contact as I crept back toward my bedroom. Since I knew it had to be church time, I avoided Daddy, hoping he would forget to herd us to the car. I couldn't imagine anything would ever keep our family from going to church on a Sunday morning. It seemed like a sin to stay in my blue stretch shorts and striped T-shirt, but I sure hoped I wouldn't have to put on my Sunday dress.

It was one of those early spring days when it's warmer outside than inside the house. The morning chill still remained, and heat blew up from the floor register in the middle of my room. As I slid down to sit against my bed, I picked up the nearby loop-weaving frame and fiddled with it as my hair snapped with static.

A little later, our minister, Reverend Nieuwsma, arrived at the house wearing a suit, tie, and shiny black loafers. Everyone was beckoned back to the living room. He preached at us from the brown overstuffed chair, one hand holding his Bible open in front of him.

The words he read reminded me of things I heard every week in Sunday school. With his free hand, he gestured with an upraised palm, "Whosoever believeth in Him, will not perish, but will have everlasting life." Pointing his forefinger upwards, he continued, "When we die and leave this earthly body, we will have a mansion on a street of gold."

I always thought these things were somehow true. *But how did a soul go to heaven without the body?* It seemed kind of scary to die and go to heaven. I wasn't sure I ever wanted to go there.

*If I went there too, would I be able to recognize my mommy in her new body? How would I know which mansion she was in?*

That afternoon the food parade began and seemed to go on for weeks. I thought Reverend Nieuwsma must have told everyone in the church to bring us meals. Cars trickled into the farmyard, carrying neighbors, friends, or relatives, who stared at us. It seemed that each woman presented a casserole dish as her offering.

One lady shook her head, saying, "Those poor kids!"

Another woman commented, "I'm so sorry for your loss. Martha was such a wonderful person!"

I wanted the procession to stop—to have things back the way they were. I reasoned that the ladies caused the chaos, and I surely didn't like the way they talked about my mommy in the past tense. I silently asked God, *If they stopped bringing casseroles, then could our lives be normal again?*

The phone sounded over and over. Three short rings on our party line constantly beckoned someone to answer. When Daddy was in the house, he picked up the receiver and gave details about my mommy's death. His words were a reminder that she could not come back.

Daddy said to a caller, "No. She was fine on Saturday, didn't complain that her heart was racing like it sometimes did. When I returned from my early morning chores, I couldn't wake her." I wondered why he didn't seem sad.

One afternoon, I watched my big sisters as they worked in the kitchen area. My legs dangled back and forth over the edge of a chair in the corner. Audrey faced me as she was perched on the clothes hamper along the opposite wall. Daddy filled his glass at the kitchen sink and turned to face his daughters. "You girls are going to school tomorrow."

"There's no way we're going back to school yet, Dad," Cindy said. "Besides, who would make the meals and clean all these eggs?" She waved an arm toward wire egg baskets and mounds of cartons that filled the table.

Eloise entered from the egg room just off the kitchen, wiping her brow with the corner of a hand towel. The egg-washing machine gurgled, the clothes washer and dryer in the kitchen splashed and whirled. Giving Daddy a glare, she shook her head from side to side. "We're not going."

Daddy drank the entire glass of water and set it down on the porcelain ledge of the sink. He didn't press the issue any further but stepped to the coat closet and silently put on his barn jacket.

I felt quivery whenever they fought because I had no choice in family decisions. Whatever my big sisters did, I had to do. It was awful enough to be where I was. I couldn't imagine having to face other people away from home. I was relieved they got their way, and we didn't go to school most of that week.

I believed my mommy was in heaven, but I couldn't understand why God wanted her there instead of with me. I thought I needed her a lot more than He did but didn't quite know how to tell Him that.

When another car pulled in the yard, I ran off to the field behind our house. This time of the year, there was flattened corn stubble and tiny weeds trying to break through the furrows of hard clay.

An uneasy hot feeling bubbled up inside of me, and I kicked a rotted ear of corn as far as I could. The way I understood my Sunday school lessons, being angry with God was a bad sin. My brothers and sisters seemed sad but not exactly mad. My sisters were often crying, and my brothers quietly went from barn to table to coop like robots.

Looking up at the blue expanse, I silently implored, *God, would you please bring her back? I promise I'll be a really good girl if you do. I won't hide from Daddy when he wants me to work in the barn, and I won't pretend I didn't hear Mommy when she tells me to sweep the kitchen.*

I recalled the naughtiest thing I ever did. When I was four, I had a play date with a little older boy named Ricky. His family rented a nearby house from my daddy. Ricky persuaded me to join him in breaking thirty-three square windows of the chicken coop in their backyard.

"It's fun," he said, handing me a tree branch. "Use this stick, and you can reach them – like this." Ricky ran as he lashed his stick. "No one will ever know. Come on!"

It seemed dangerous but exciting when I followed him around one side of the coop and then the other. He knocked out the top ones, and I broke the bottom ones. Splintered panes cracked a second time when they fell onto the cement foundation.

When I stood in our back-porch doorway as the window episode was exposed, my mommy raised her head from the pot on the stove, and her disappointed eyes met mine. I don't remember my final punishment. That look was all I needed.

Walking in the field now three years later, I promised God I would never knock out windows again. But I couldn't take it back. The deal didn't seem to change His mind.

# Chapter 4

# Words of Love

*Let love and faithfulness never leave you; bind them around your neck, write them on the tablet of your heart.*
Proverbs 3:3

Three days after Mommy died, Eloise called me into the house. She stayed home most of the time, those first couple of weeks. She and Cindy, at the ages of eighteen and fifteen, suddenly took over all Mommy's chores. They prepared meals, packed eggs, cleaned the house, did laundry, and greeted all the visitors.

I was summoned to the kitchen to meet my Sunday school teacher, Mrs. Miskotten, who brought me a black Bible from my Sunday school class. She wrote inside the front cover, "For Myrna, when your mom went to be with Jesus in heaven," and signed the names of each one of the kids. My mommy taught me to be nice, so I thanked her and smiled the best I could. As soon as she went to her car, I slipped back outside.

Another day, Jane, one of my best friends from school, came over with her mom and dad. My sisters and I assembled, standing around the kitchen table with them. Mr. Smart knew my sisters because he was their band teacher in our local high school. They brought letters from the children in my second-grade class, which the teacher, Mrs. Miller, had instructed them to write. On those yellowish-gray, lined pages, the kids wrote, "I'm sorry your mom died" or "We're studying magnets."

They all chatted above our heads as I shuffled through some of the papers. When Eloise's eyes met mine, I cut in to thank them for bringing the letters. I forced a shy half-smile at Jane. This week seemed to separate me from my friends—now we were a universe apart. I was the girl whose mom died.

A regular hobby of mine was to find construction paper, cupcake liners, bits of foil, glue, and crayons. I gathered the materials on the kitchen table and worked diligently on love notes to my mommy. On one of her birthdays, I folded a red paper in half, and wrote loving words on the front. "For Mommy, Happy Birthday." I glued on a yellow cupcake liner to resemble a flower, and on the inside of the card wrote, "I love you! To Mommy, From Myrna." When she was close by, I stood up a couple of books to hide my project. We both grinned slyly until she left the kitchen.

When I was finished making the card, I set it up on the kitchen counter, right in front of the radio. Mommy wouldn't miss it because she listened to a local talk show, *Talk of the Town*, and news all morning and reached for glasses and coffee cups in the cupboard directly above. It was her first stop every time she walked into the room.

Later, when Mommy went back into the kitchen, I tiptoed from the dining room, to peek around the doorframe and held my mouth to contain a giggle. Mommy looked down from the card to find my eyes. We laughed as I ran to her. She held me in a long embrace.

The best notes of all were the words my mommy wrote and received. I remember times late at night when I snuck out of bed to find her sitting in a comfortable chair in our dining room in the flickering blue light of the TV. She usually waited up for my oldest siblings to come home from dates or school events. The exhausted farmer's wife and mother of six would not allow sleep until she made time to write a letter and fill a page in her diary. Our dining room didn't contain a table, just a few easy chairs facing a television set. Communication with relatives and friends was important to her. A bundle of stationery, recently received letters, and her diary were stored in a nearby drawer in the bureau.

Mommy didn't tell me to get back in bed. She held me in the crook of her left arm, while she detailed her day with her fountain pen, holding the brown leather book on the flat right side of the white vinyl chair. As she dipped her pen, the musty smell of the ink in the jar wafted up from the nearby windowsill. The warmth of her body, the beat of her heart, and the softness of her nightgown made my eyelids heavy.

She wrote a page in her little diary book every day of her life beginning at age fourteen. Each New Year's Day, for thirty-three years, one more volume was placed inside her cedar chest to soak up the sweet aroma along with her silky white wedding dress, and blankets she knitted for her babies.

# Chapter 5

# Searching and Finding

> *"Then you will call on me and come and pray to me, and I will listen to you. You will seek me and find me when you seek me with all your heart. I will be found by you," declares the LORD.* Jeremiah 29:12–14

When Jane and her parents left our house that day, I looked for Mommy in my big brother's bedroom this time, up one of the two stairways. Lingering at the doorway of Ron's silent room, I imagined what it would be like if my mommy were putting clean sheets on his bed.

She would've smiled my way, saying, "How was school today, Myrna? Would you grab that corner and give it a tug?"

*Maybe if I searched the whole house and farm, I would find her.*

Family sing-alongs around the piano were common in my childhood. We stood while my mommy played familiar hymns and Sunday school songs. I slipped through my siblings to position myself on the bench next to Mommy. My heart was full when we sang together. She'd often narrate our performances. Sometimes when Daddy pressed the green button on the reel-to-reel tape recorder, these sessions were preserved for the future. When we searched our minds for the memory of my mom's voice many years later, we were blessed to be able to press play on modern technology to find it. Her voice could warm our hearts again.

As the first days unfolded immediately after my mommy's death, I woke up in the mornings hoping it had been a bad dream, and I would discover her doing household chores. But same as the day before, the sad story was true.

The week after mommy died, I wandered all the way back to the Pretty Place. The legendary spot in the woods behind our house was so named because it was like an outdoor sanctuary. Everyone in my family knew about it, but it was a place to retreat, hide, cry, or just be alone. The walk took about fifteen minutes. Just before entering the Pretty Place, there were a handful of branches to pull to the side. It was like stepping out of the wardrobe in Narnia into another world.

At the top of the ridge, I could see the creek flowing from the left side and curling around in front of me, continuing on to the right and beyond. The woodsy smell of water filled my senses. Often, I performed my Sunday school songs or radio hits to the audience of trees and wildflowers. Sometimes I sat silently on a large tree root to soak in the green beauty and listen to the bubbling creek as it raced down to parts unknown. I didn't comprehend it then, but the Lord was certainly speaking to me in His still, small voice, infusing His presence into my heart.

When I left the Pretty Place, I felt refreshed and filled with hope to deal with my sorrows. I knew intuitively the Holy Spirit was indwelling me, although at that age, I didn't know how to name the experience. The God of peace filled me with strength for each day.

I didn't find my mommy on earth, but the Lord Jesus found a way into my heart for life.

# Chapter 6

# What Will Happen to Me?

*"For I know the plans I have for you,"* declares the LORD, "plans to prosper you and not to harm you, plans to give you hope and a future."
Jeremiah 29:11

I began overhearing conversations and thought I heard people say, "What about Audrey and Myrna?" I thought the same thing . . . *What about us?* The comments within the family, and from visitors often referred to Audrey and me. As I wandered around the house and farmyard those first few weeks, my ears perked up when they mentioned our names. I don't remember anyone saying that particular word, but it was firmly in my mind. *Orphanage.*

My second-grade brain pondered this. There were still five of us children at home, but things were changing fast. My second to the oldest brother, John, had married Sherry and was around twenty-one years old. My oldest brother Ron, who was twenty-four, had plans to be married in June. My oldest sister Eloise, the third child, was eighteen, dating boys, and working as a waitress. I thought it wouldn't be long until she moved out of the house. That left the youngest three of us. Cindy, the fourth child, was fifteen but seemed so much older. She worked on part-time jobs, was intensely independent, and was also ready to do grown-up things. Disturbing thoughts entered my mind about who would take care of Audrey and me.

I had never heard of anyone who didn't have a mom in my class at our little school. Kids told tales about neglected children with dirty faces and ragged clothes. Nobody sat down and explained anything to me. They all seemed so busy. I knew my daddy cared for me, but he was a man with a huge farm to run. He certainly wouldn't read to me or hug me goodnight at bedtime. My daddy didn't share his thoughts or emotions with us, so confusion and assumptions formed. Without my mommy there, I couldn't imagine our family being able to function. She was the one who held me on her lap late at night, and she was gone.

I wondered if Cindy would stay on the farm and make meals for my dad. I wondered if Audrey and I would even get to stay together when we went to another place? I thought if I brought it up, then someone might come to take me to one of those places. Maybe if we just didn't tell *those* people, then *they* wouldn't know about me. I sensed I should keep my head down and bide my time.

When ladies came over, they spoke in muffled voices to my daddy using phrases like "poor little kids." Someone mentioned that my mommy was only forty-seven years old. In second grade in 1969, we didn't talk about how old our moms were. I hadn't known her age; I only knew she was mine.

A frequent retreat for me was to our garage, a beat-up building behind the house that hadn't contained cars for years. I passed the dilapidated pool table to pull the string that turned on the inverted bulb hanging there. As I balanced a chipped bowl filled with milk and bread, I climbed the wooden slats to the loft where many of my cats' homes were.

When one of them looked fat with baby kitties, I made soft beds for them with burlap bags tucked into wooden peach boxes. Mother cats trusted me to quietly witness the birth of the helpless sacs as I sat breathlessly between glass chick waterers and discarded tractor parts. The smell of truck oil, dust, and milk mingled in my nostrils.

My cats didn't mind if I sang them one of my Sunday school songs. "A sunbeam, a sunbeam, I'll be a sunbeam for Him!" The light bulb glowed, forming a semicircle on the ceiling up in our loft.

# Chapter 7

## Patent Leather Traditions

*Know therefore that the LORD your God is God; he is the faithful God, keeping his covenant of love to a thousand generations of those who love him and keep his commandments.* Deuteronomy 7:9

Wandering around the farm, I thought about the last night Mommy was alive. After my Saturday night bath, she put me to bed and read me a book as usual. As she sat on the side of my bed, she placed one hand on my arm, and the other hand on the opposite shoulder. Mommy listened to my normal prayer. "Now I lay me down to sleep, I pray the Lord my soul to keep, if I should die before I wake, I pray the Lord my soul to take, Amen." After our embrace, she lingered in my doorway a few moments and took a couple bobby pins out of her hair. She left them on top of my bookcase. In hopes she might come back to look for them, I didn't move them for months.

We all had to leave our house and face throngs of people at visitations and a funeral that week. Reality was setting in. People said she was in heaven.

At the funeral visitation, my sister Audrey and I stood between Cindy and Eloise, all in our Sunday best. Hundreds of people came to pay their respects. The line curled around two sides of the funeral home building into the parking lot. The tradition in our small Dutch town was such that the family and the community members stayed in lines. The visitors shook hands with every one of the family members as they progressed through. The lines remained intact.

The most common remark from visitors was, "I'm so sorry, you poor children." Many of them hugged us and couldn't hold back their tears. I wondered, *Was I supposed to try to comfort these older people?*

Mommy's father, Grandpa John Volkema, stood guard near her open casket for all the visitation hours. When the line diminished and we were about to go home, Grandpa began to sing a Dutch hymn. We all sat down and stared off into our own worlds while he sang. He had already lost another daughter, my aunt Bertha, several years before, and now his oldest daughter went on to heaven ahead of him. He was acquainted with many painful losses and trials in his life. This very stoic Dutchman displayed a rare show of emotion as the pain oozed out in the whiny slow tune.

A couple weeks later, my big sisters took Audrey and me to downtown Holland to buy new clothes for Easter. Daddy passed the checkbook to Eloise and off we went to the Eighth Street stores. Mommy would have been with us to purchase dresses, sweaters, shoes, lacy socks, purses and hats. My items were mostly white with splashes of pastels. My mommy would have laid egg money down on the counter for extra items like new hankies or Necco candy wafers for church. It was the way things were done in the late sixties. The tradition of new Easter outfits was a legacy we felt compelled to carry on even though this year we walked slower, and our eyes lacked twinkle.

On Easter morning my mommy would have tied the bow on the back of my dress and buckled my white patent leather shoes as my daddy placed dimes and nickels on the kitchen table for our collection in Sunday School. This bright Easter morning, we grabbed the black metal handrail as we stepped carefully down the back-porch stairs to avoid scuffs on our new white shoes.

A snapshot captured my daddy's four girls lined up in front of the green 1968 Ford. We forced the corners of our mouths upward while our gloved hands held our Bibles and purses.

# Chapter 8

# Delayed Grief

*You will keep in perfect peace those whose minds are steadfast, because they trust in you.* Isaiah 26:3

When I was middle-aged, I spent an evening in the hospital to support a family member who, like me, has Long QT syndrome. It's a heart defect, which you can have without any problems, or it can create enough havoc to warrant a defibrillator and medications. Both of us are genetically diagnosed as having it, but we don't normally have any issues.

My mom most likely died from complications of the defect, but it wasn't identified yet, and we didn't know its name in those days. Many years later, we learned a great deal about it.

After several hours at the hospital that evening, the doctor determined my family member could go home and follow up with their own cardiologist. On the highway that dark rainy night, during the long drive home, I prayed out loud all the way.

When I reached the country road only a few miles from home, I was suddenly overtaken with heavy sobbing to the point I had to pull the car off to the side of the road. My mom had already been gone over forty years, but that night it hit me all over again.

I was in travail and experienced something like a vision at the same time. In my mind, I was in the farmhouse shortly after my mom's death. I cried out, "Mom, Mom! Mom!" The crying kept coming over me in waves that threatened to drown me.

Much later, I calmed down enough to finish the drive home. Again, I felt the strong call from God to write about my mom's death. God didn't speak in human words, but I knew in my spirit He was encouraging me to share my story.

Since that night, I've learned from professionals that the crying and vision I experienced was most likely delayed grief. It can happen to a person many years after a death, and it usually happens after another circumstance, which is the trigger. For some reason, a person needs to again grieve the event that happened many years ago.

As a child, I often felt abandoned and afraid like during that sobbing episode, but I knew my mom didn't deliberately leave me. Even at a young age, I knew deep down in my soul that she wouldn't leave me on purpose. I wondered again why my mom had to die so young.

Years after my mom passed away, when other painful things occurred, I asked the same question. It felt like I had a deep cut that bleeds again when it gets bumped a little too hard. By my late teens, I knew something good must come out of this great trial.

# Chapter 9

# Our God of Hope

*May the God of hope fill you with all joy and peace as you trust in him, so that you may overflow with hope by the power of the Holy Spirit.*
Romans 15:13

Living life alone was difficult for my dad. He married again six months after my mom died. Soon two more of my siblings got married, my parents became grandparents, and each of us was very busy with school, work, and farm life. My family underwent many changes, joys, heartaches, and deaths throughout the following years.

My teenage years were awkward as most experience, but deep sorrow was added. Eight years after my mom, my sister Audrey also died unexpectedly in her sleep when she was eighteen years old. Much later, it was assumed that she also died of the Long QT Syndrome. One of my brothers had a horrible farming accident that nearly took his life. Later my first stepmother died of cancer. All of this happened by the time I was eighteen.

During my college years, my dad married a third time. By then, all of us children were much more mature, and the circumstances were completely different. My siblings and I were grown, with our own lives to live. In the later years of my dad's life, I began to understand more about him.

My dad was brought up to work hard in the era of the Great Depression, when life was so difficult. As an only child, he had to take over the farm and care for his ailing mother at age eighteen when his father died suddenly after a horse accident. He learned to keep going, hold his feelings inside, and to press on no matter what happened. My dad didn't express emotions of grief or sadness. I never received a hug or an "I love you" from him, but he loved his family fiercely by acts of service. He was a provider.

In the following years, I married, taught elementary school for twenty-seven years, had two sons, and lived a productive, busy life. The physical, emotional, and spiritual challenges were great at times when I struggled with anxiety or physical illnesses. Individual and corporate prayer became so important during spiritual warfare. There were high points when I felt close to God and low valleys when I thought my prayers were not being heard. The Lord brought me back around every time. I was the one who moved; He remained constant.

The Holy Spirit of God comforted me through my childhood, teen, and adult years. He walked with me through the waving wheat and the airy gullies. God showed up in the form of teachers, high school girlfriends, stepmothers, Bible study groups, sisters, church friends, a mother-in-law, pastors, lifetime best friends, my husband, and within nature. He never let go of me. God worked through people and circumstances of my life to shower love on me. Even when I doubted His plans and methods were the best, He held me up with His righteous right hand.

I didn't know when, but I knew the Holy Spirit would lead me to tell the world of God's faithfulness even through the fires and storms of life.

What Jesus Christ did for us by His death and resurrection secured salvation for believers. I have the blessed assurance of heaven, where I will see my mom. That's true hope from our God of Hope.

Myrna, one week old, with her mom, Martha, and sister, Audrey

Myrna, eleven weeks old, and mom, Martha, with sisters Audrey and Cindy

Myrna, nine months old, with mom, Martha, enjoying the farm cats

Myrna, thirteen months old, with mom, Martha

Myrna, two years old, with mom, Martha, and sister, Audrey

Myrna, age four, in 1966. All six Kleinheksel siblings,
(L to R) Myrna, John, Eloise, Cindy, Ron, Audrey.
The farmhouse and swing board are in the background

Myrna, age four, with mom, Martha, and sister, Audrey, 1966

Myrna, age five, in 1967, holding onto her mom, Martha. Includes Grandpa Volkema, (mom's dad), Myrna's dad, Gordon, and sister Audrey

Myrna, age seven, with sisters, Audrey and Eloise in their Sunday best for Easter, 1969, two weeks after mom died

Myrna Folkert

# OTHER WOMEN'S STORIES

# YOUNGER THAN TWENTY WHEN MOM DIED

# Chapter 10

# Journaling was a Friend

# With Marie Getz

*Marie was thirty-nine at the time of the interview.
She was eighteen in 1996 when her mom, Gayle,
died at the age of forty-two.*

My mom had rheumatoid arthritis, but she suddenly had even more pain, causing my parents to seek specialists. She had been declining for some time, and they didn't know why. She was very uncomfortable and couldn't walk. A CT scan revealed she had cancer, which had spread to the marrow of her spine, invading so fast that it was already too late to treat her.

My mom was in a hospital bed in our living room for her last months, and we took care of her there. She had the death rattle in her throat and didn't speak the last few days. We sang some favorite hymns to her, "How Great Thou Art" and "How Firm a Foundation." My sister and I were there when she died early in the morning. Later, the mortician came to put her on a stretcher, covered her up with a bag, and took her away. I was far removed from reality at the time and wasn't processing my feelings.

My mom had a deep faith. We often saw her reading the Bible or on her knees praying. My mom loved people well, mentored others, and was an outgoing person, which is amazing considering all she struggled with inside. She was spurred on to seek God, because she grew up with deep hurts from childhood abuse. The demons of her past bothered her, and she dealt with it by overeating, which makes me suspect she had an undiagnosed eating disorder. She buried her feelings and never dealt with them. At times she made comments to me about eating less although I was very thin. I didn't know about her abuse until after her death when my dad told me.

Even before my mom got diagnosed, I wasn't handling my emotions well and developed eating disorders. I'm sure my mom knew, but she didn't discuss it with me. I was an angry, rebellious teen, and then on top of that, my parents took my brother and sister and me out of school to homeschool us in my ninth-grade year. Anger grew in me, and I was even mad at God. My parents were searching for another church when they began to homeschool, so we didn't have any close connections with other people.

Because of all the demons my mom had, she was miserable. Later in my teen years, I watched her come to peace, as she changed from a sarcastic, aggressive person to a person of acceptance, healing, and forgiveness. The Lord showed her how to be submissive to her husband and not hurt people with her words. She was open about that and shared her testimony with others. One of her favorite Bible verses was James 2:13, about how mercy triumphs over judgment. Instead of the negative in her life, she tried to show us the opposite. She badly wanted us to come to peace with God too, like all Christian parents do for their kids, but I resisted. Because I experienced the way she was before, it threw me into a whirlwind.

My mom wasn't able to do many physical things with us because of her arthritis. She always took time at night to sit on the edge of my bed to listen and talk with me. She made a big deal of birthdays too, so now I do that with my family. My mom taught me to keep going, no matter what and take care of your family. She was in mental and physical torment with rheumatoid arthritis ever since my brother was born, but she kept going. I see that determination in myself, and I'm happy about that. It's God's grace in my life, and it was in hers too. She was an excellent mother, always putting us first, to the detriment of her own health. A healthy balance is hard to achieve. In church we're taught to die to self. We often give all of ourselves.

During this time, I had guilt because I couldn't think outside of myself. Even though my sister was two years younger than me, she was able to go with the flow. I wasn't angry with her though, and we remain best friends to this day. My brother, who is seven years younger than me, was only ten, and struggled for years, but he is doing well now. Siblings can have the same experience and react so differently. As a young child, I came to know the Lord, but as a teenager, I confronted my parents' decisions and acted negatively towards them. After she found out about her spreading cancer, my mom didn't accept the fact that she was dying. We were a part of a church that taught if you had enough faith, you would be healed. I was in a fog with my selfish thinking and completely blocked out much of what was going on. I was close to my mom when I was young, but later I wasn't close to her at all. Strangely though, I think my mom and I understood one another better than anyone else in the family. It could have been because of our shared emotional difficulties, though I didn't know at the time about her many scars from her childhood.

My mom's death was followed by funeral visitations. They were painful because there were so many people around, and I just wanted to be alone. I found it all so upsetting. Many comments people made were so empty. At the funeral we sang some songs. The pastor spoke about my mom. I blanked out the whole day, and actually feel like I blanked out several years. Maybe because of my own negative frame of mind, for a long time I was ashamed for my feelings. Now I know my feelings were okay. God helped me through, and He has restored like He says in scripture.

In the months following her death, we were offered counseling and grieving classes, but sadly, my dad was from that generation who thought only people in terrible situations did counseling and he didn't let us go. It would have made a world of difference. About five years after my mom died, I spiraled down into depression even further. I wanted to die. Many times, during my teenage years, I suffered from depression, which led to self-hatred. Only by God's grace, He sustained me that I didn't kill myself. I'm a cautious firstborn, so the plans were very passive.

After some time, my dad finally saw some of this and helped me get counseling. I was barely surviving, eating and purging. My dad thought the counselor gave terrible advice, so I was only able to go a few times. It was amazing to be able to talk with someone who was completely removed. Counseling was like a massage for my soul.

When my husband and I dated in my twenties, I was still struggling through a rough period in my life. My pride and intense desire to look like I had it all together prevented people from knowing my misery. After my marriage, in my late twenties, I began to open up my heart and feel love again. It was a relief. Having our first baby, who's nine now, helped in that process, but then I was terrified. I didn't want to love too deeply for fear the other person might die. God has helped me by showing me how much I can trust Him and how good He is. A few years ago, I went for more counseling sessions. Just this year, when I was singing and praying with the Lord, it was the first time I could look at a picture of myself and say, "I forgive you."

I've struggled in my own parenting. Without even knowing it, I was doing and saying negative things. My wise husband helps me to make good decisions. I have asked God to show me areas to improve so my children won't struggle when they're my age. I'm learning more positive ways to handle things, and I want to continue going forward. My husband often mentions the Bible verse, "A soft answer turns away wrath."

I didn't have a mentor when I was younger, but I think most of that was my own doing. I pushed people away, my friends, and later, even my husband. My relationship with him was shallow and not as rich as it could have been. Recently we've realized this and are working on developing more closeness.

A couple years ago, the Lord brought me a mentor, who has helped me with these struggles. She's an eighty-five-year-old dear friend who shows me His love. I met her at a fundraiser for a camp she helps to organize, which is for children who have parents with addictions. The Lord had revealed to me that I was addicted to striving to fix myself on my own. The fact that my mom died in February, and the amount of dark days at that time of year, makes winter a time when I'm susceptible to depression. My mentor asked me to lead at the children's camp occasionally. I didn't feel qualified at all, but then thought about all those prophets in the Bible, like Jonah, who didn't obey God. My mentor is pleased with the progress I'm making to see outside of myself and be more in touch with my feelings. I'm so thankful the Lord placed her in my life.

I wish I had talked to my mom about many more things. I wish I knew about her life, what she went through, and how she transformed into who she was later on. You don't realize how much you want to talk to your parents until you become a parent yourself. I'm happy my mom is with God, but I wish she could have shared my life and known my kids. I've reconnected with one of her sisters, my aunt, and she has been able to fill in some holes for me.

My family and I recently visited the town my mom died in, and we saw the house and the gravestone. It's my desire my children know about their Grandma Gayle, so I explained things to them as we saw the places. It was the first time in many years that I had visited, and it gave me peace.

If I could, I would ask her, "Would you forgive me?" I'd ask forgiveness for my rotten attitude and how I treated her badly in my teenage years, but I know her answer. I had a good mom. I'm sure she forgave me back then. We do that for our kids. When I became a mom, I understood that.

Journaling was a friend. I often wrote when I was young, and still do today. With extensive journaling over many years, I found closure. It was twenty-one years ago now. I was floundering and wanted to take myself out. But the Lord kept me. When women lose their mothers, my advice is to talk about it and write about it. Talking and writing are genius.

Because I've seen the depths of despair, my hope is in the Lord of peace. Now I have three kids, and I pray that I am a good mother to them and give them hope. I pray I would show His love to them, and they'd do the same to others. I want them to love fully and know they are fully loved.

It's meaningful to talk about my mom again and the events surrounding that time in my life. You have to keep talking about it, and the validation of feelings is a great way of coping. I loved my mom and to be able to talk with somebody about her is a treasure.

Bible Verses:

*But our citizenship is in heaven. And we eagerly await a Savior from there, the Lord Jesus Christ, who, by the power that enables him to bring everything under his control, will transform our lowly bodies so that they will be like his glorious body.* Philippians 3:20–21

*He went and took the scroll from the right hand of him who sat on the throne. And when he had taken it, the four living creatures and the twenty-four elders fell down before the Lamb. Each had a harp and they were holding golden bowls full with incense, which are the prayers of God's people.* Revelation 5:7–8

I love that our prayers are heard and are even in bowls of gold by the throne of God! Even in the dark times of grief, He hears us!

# Chapter 11

# Mama Ran her Fingers Through my Hair

## With Mary Sterenberg

*Mary was fifty-eight at the time of the interview. She was eighteen years old, in 1976, when her mom, Hermina, "Buni," died at the age of fifty-four.*

One weekend, when I was one month into my freshman year at Calvin College, I stayed overnight at my older sister's house. When I woke in the morning, my sister told me mom had passed away during the night.

When I was a child, before my mom got sick, I said to my little friends that if my mom died, I could never function. When it did happen, God's power gave me the grace to take one day at a time. He helped me, because she died, and I survived.

My mom wasn't one to play with me, but we spent natural time together cooking, baking, and sewing. My dad kept a promise to my mom, to take her to see the world. They lived in Montana, California, then the Netherlands and Australia for some years. They traveled much of Europe before returning to West Michigan. Most families don't get to go to Australia, especially a pastor's family. We traveled through Europe on our return to Michigan when I was eight years old.

I have a memory of knowing my mom's deep love. Since I was the youngest, when we rode in the car, I would sit on the hump and of course we didn't have seat belts then. I laid my head on my mama's lap. She would gently run her fingers through my hair. That is a touch that I love to this day. She also would hold a map up in the window of the car to prevent the sun from shining on me. I thought, *Doesn't she get tired of holding her hand up?* The biggest thing my mom taught me was selflessness. I'm not nearly as good at it as she was. I was told, even when I was born, she apologized to the doctor that he was missing his supper.

My mom lived her faith quietly as a background person. I'm not like her in that way; I'm a leader in the church. She was kind-hearted, and lovingly served others. She didn't fit the typical pastor's wife mold. She allowed me to help teach her Sunday school class when I was around ten, and I have a picture of us together. That was also the year I accepted Jesus as my Lord and Savior. She often had a Bible open and read and prayed. She lived Christlikeness.

When I was in eighth grade, I didn't make the cheerleading team and was informed in an embarrassing and hurtful way. My mom waited for me to cross the street from school to home. I came home sobbing. She just held me and cried with me and was hurt too because I was wounded.

I wonder if my mom had any regrets in her life. I know she longed for more education. She married my dad very young after he served in the military. She made the decision to marry my dad, knowing she had to take on the role of a pastor's wife. She couldn't go on to college because they began to have their large family.

Even though she wasn't highly educated, she had exquisite taste. Her sister worked at an expensive department store, and the girls got fine clothing at a huge discount. My mom still wore fine things when she married a preacher. They certainly didn't have much money, but she always looked classy. She wore an elegant gray and red suit in her casket.

Over the years, I realized my family was protecting me too much and not telling me things when my mom was passing away, so I have worked on making sure our family had much more open communication. I have diamond earrings from my boyfriend, my husband now, which he gave to me when mom was dying because he knew it was important to me. My mom always wanted diamond earrings but never got them. I begged my siblings and dad to get them for her, but they said, "She doesn't care anymore." Maybe that was me not fully understanding she wasn't going to be around.

The day after she died, I went with my dad and sisters to pick out the casket. My dad wanted a casket that had an open Bible imprinted in the satin inside. He said, "Because the Word of God was so important to her." That made sense because it also communicated to me of my father's wishes that she be remembered for the preciousness of the Word of God.

I was very emotional at the visitations. A relative came up to me and tried to shush me, saying, "It's all right. You'll be just fine." It was definitely a message of, "Don't cry." She made me feel bad for crying. I was thinking, *I'm supposed to cry, my mom just died!* There was some of that crazy mindset of, *We are Christian Reformed, and we don't cry and show our emotions.*

The funeral visitations were so exhausting. It seemed the entire community came. My dad and mom were so well-known and loved. My dad was a pastor in Grand Haven in a Christian Reformed Church.

It's a miracle I went into healing prayer in my pastoring, because I have some bad memories about that concerning my mom. A group of people came to pray over my mom when she was sick, but she still died. Later they made it clear to us that she died because we didn't have enough faith. Satan would have wanted me to be angry and not go into healing prayer ministry.

Now in my pastoring, I will never tell anyone their loved one died because they didn't have enough faith. I'm super sensitive to that, and I think it was a good lesson. I believe God allows suffering for the greater good. We never know His purposes, He is sovereign, and He is in control. What I want is one thing, but maybe God has another plan. People are not always healed on this earth. He says ask, so I'm going to ask in faith for healing. I know completely and fully that He heals! He chose to take my mama when she was fifty-four. I don't know why. I have truly missed having my mom in my life.

When we drove away in the hearse after the funeral, I looked out the window at my friends and wasn't able to smile at them when we caught eyes with each other. That struck me because I'm a smiler. The procession of cars from Grand Haven to Grand Rapids was a couple miles long.

One night after my mom's death, I was beside myself with grief, and my husband now, Bruce, and my sister came to my college dorm to help me. I couldn't understand why God took my mom. *Why would He do such a thing?* I thought I was going crazy. Then my sister told me a story I never knew. I knew I was a premature baby, born four weeks early, but she told me my mom almost died the night I was born. My mom prayed she would live long enough to see all her children grown. One month after I went to college, she died. Tell me, did God take my mother, or did He give me a mother for eighteen years? That changed my whole perspective. My mom could have never been there at all for me. That truth got me through, and I'll never forget it. I'm a different person because of the story my sister told me that night.

My mom wanted all of us to have a college degree, which she was never able to get. I'm sure I made the right decision to stay in college, even though some thought I should stay home to take care of my dad after she died.

She was refined in her taste and loved music, especially the oratorio, Handel's Messiah. It is all very scriptural, and the words are straight out of the Bible. She dreamed that I would sing in it. I finally sang in it the December after she died and sang in it for the following ten years in honor of my mom.

When I planned my wedding, I did it by myself, with some help from my sister, who is ten years older, and a roommate who was also getting married. My sister and her husband, Jack, played an important role, but they were still more like siblings than parents to me. I wore my mom's wedding veil at my wedding. My daughter-in-law carried my mom's white Bible down the aisle when she married my son, just as my mom did when she married my dad. My dad took the diamonds out of the wedding ring set he gave my mom. Then he had a necklace with a tiny diamond made for each of my sisters and me.

You know how scents remind you of people? I have this container of Great Lady perfume, almost full, which reminds me of my mom. I don't use it; it's mom's scent.

I regret that I mistreated my mother-in-law when we were first married. She said things like, "I know you don't have your mother, but I'll be here." I didn't want a replacement. She was just trying to be caring and fill that void. She's gone now too.

My dad did remarry, but not until four years after my mom's death. My children always had Grandma Carolyn as the grandma they knew. I longed for them to know my mom, but they never missed out on having a grandma. My mother-in-law and grandma were also around a lot of years, so my children had excellent grandmothers.

If you're a grieving daughter, I would say, no one will ever fill the place of your mother. That place will always stay vacant. Time heals, but you'll always miss your mother. It hit me today, I was crying just before this interview. I still miss my mother.

Your mom has a huge impact on who you are. I know my mom didn't have good self-esteem and that transferred to me. I had healing prayer for that, and now I feel good about myself. I have talked to my children about anxieties I might have passed onto them. Now those have healed too. I have two sons and a daughter who have grown to be amazing adults, and they are now parents themselves. Now we have six grandchildren.

I miss my mom in normal daily things. I longed for my parents to be at my recent seminary graduation. Every October 11, I remember my mom on her death date. There's something about the changing leaves. It was a very windy day at her graveside service with leaves swirling about. There's a whole process of beauty within death. The leaves are dying, yet it's in their death they're beautiful. Then they fall off, and we have this ugliness again as we go through winter, but there's new life every spring, with buds. Her death feels ugly, but then the spring comes. There's something about her dying in October that reminds me of a natural life-cycle rhythm. That process brings me comfort. I love the fall colors, and they always speak to me about God.

A mother is the one who holds the family together. Somehow the responsibility of getting our family together has fallen to me. We have a very large home, and it's important to me, so we are the hosts of most get-togethers. Someone is needed to carry the role to keep a family together if the mother isn't there, or they will separate.

When at a recent funeral, the grandchildren of the deceased spoke about their loving relationship with their grandparents. I hope my grandchildren know they are loved and know the Savior through me. I didn't have my mom to pass herself on that way for my kids. We knew our grandparents, but we had to sit in a chair and be still when we were at their house. I've maybe gone too far the other way, but I spoil our grandchildren, play with them, and buy them way too many toys.

I lead a "back to the womb" prayer when I teach at conferences or meet with people. I learned it from Francis and Judith McNutt. We ask the Lord about getting to the source of the pain people have. We take them back to the sanctified imagination about their life in the womb of their mother. We ask them to think about things like how mom felt while she was pregnant with them, or the fourth month when she got punched in the gut causing terrible pain. It's amazing what the Lord reveals to help people. Before I did it with others, I took myself through the process. Much inner healing occurs, and I've seen God do a lot of miracles.

My family will be reunited again in glory. Right now, is just a tiny piece compared to eternity with Jesus Christ our Lord. It feels lonesome to be separated from the ones we love now but think about eternity with Him and having our spirits reconnected.

It's been forty years since my mama died and honestly, I don't take the time to think about her very often anymore, so it was precious to tell her story. That's another thing I tell others – don't stuff it, bring the memories to the surface. I remind people, if you don't talk about it, you won't have it. We carry part of our parents' DNA, but you need to make an effort to keep the memories alive. It's good to remember.

Bible Verses:

*Blessed are those who fear the LORD . . . Surely the righteous will never be shaken; they will be remembered forever.* Psalm 112:1, 6

*Truly my soul finds rest in God; my salvation comes from him. Truly he is my rock and my salvation; he is my fortress; I will never be shaken.* Psalm 62:1–2

This was illuminated to me by the Spirit when I was young—God chose me, and I knew Jesus as my Savior.

# Chapter 12

## Escape from Sudan

## With Rebecca Deng

*Rebecca was thirty years old at the time of the interview. She was only two years old, in 1987, when her mom, Achol, died at the age of twenty-two years old, in Southern Sudan.*

My grandmother took care of me and raised me in my early childhood after my mom died. Our village, Duk, in Southern Sudan, was attacked by North Sudan. The south had mostly traditional Christian believers, and the north was largely Muslim. They were fighting for years, and often the north came to burn our village down. At the time of one of the attacks, my family and I had to take off running.

As my grandmother, my mother, and I were running, my mother went into labor in the wilderness, and died during the delivery of my sibling. Soon the baby also died. There were no nearby hospitals to help in any way. I didn't see my mother die, as my grandmother sheltered me from seeing disturbing things as much as possible. My mom, Achol, was twenty-two, and I was only two years old.

After a couple weeks, my grandmother and I attempted to live in our village again. From age two to five, I was with my grandmother. My father was a military commander fighting on the frontlines of the battlefield in the northern villages and only made it home occasionally to check on us.

My grandmother protected me from the common destinies for young girls—kidnapping, given into the sex trade, raised as a dowry for a marriage by age thirteen, or dying during the war.

In 1992 when I was about six, there was another attack on our village of Duk. I left with my uncle, his wife, some cousins, and other children who lost their parents. I'm the only child in my family who was born to my mother. I do have some stepsiblings I never knew. My aged grandmother didn't feel up to the journey, so she didn't come along. We walked for months and months, hoping to find help and relief.

On our journey, often, our temporary churches were bombed. The adults constructed a church on a site as we traveled. The government bombed it, and the next Saturday they built another grass church. This happened over and over. My bed of very thin sheets wasn't heavy enough to keep me warm during the cold nights in the camp. We walked during the hot days. I was very afraid because wild animals like lions, snakes, and crocodiles hurt or ate some people. Hunger was always knocking. Soldiers often took advantage of women and girls.

After many months, we arrived at a refugee camp in Kenya. Some children from my little village ended up staying there too. When I was around eight years old, some other relatives made their way to the refugee camp and relayed the news about the deaths of my grandmother and dad. They thought my grandmother had died from a disease that was common during the war. I never had any correspondence with my grandmother after I left our village. My dad died while fighting in the military.

The process began to send lost boys to America. Many of them went to Ethiopia first, on their way to the US. The case was made in Congress, or Homeland Security, to approve education and adoption for these boys by American families. People scattered during the war and escaped to any country that would accept them. There were around three thousand boys and eighty-nine girls that I'm aware of that came through Kenya. Many went to other countries, got kidnapped, got married very young, or didn't make it out of the war. When you make it out, you know it was only by God's grace.

We heard about a program that allowed children to come to the United States to attend school if you didn't have a mom or a dad. Since I qualified, I went to the UN office in Kenya with a translator to fill out paperwork. In our culture, girls were not normally allowed to travel alone, but my uncle and aunt weren't able to help me, so I was on my own. When I was fifteen years old, I left Kenya through this program in the year 2000.

I often think about my mother. I'm glad she influenced me as a very small child. I don't even have a picture of her and can't remember what she looks like. When death happens in a war, everything happens so abruptly. That's the hardest part for me. It's one thing when you grieve someone, but it's another thing when it happens with no warning. We know death will happen, but I feel lost because of not being able to know her or say goodbye to her. I think the most traumatizing part for me is not having a tomb to visit to honor my mom. Since everything happened so fast, and when I was very young, I never had a chance to have a childhood.

My grandma told me my mother was a wonderful and kind Christian woman. I know she had the Christian faith because of what she and my father stood for against the Muslims in the war with northern Sudan. I only knew my mother through what my grandmother told me.

When I arrived in the US, I was pregnant as a result of something that happened to me in the refugee camp. We found out I was with child shortly after coming here, and my foster parents were very understanding. My daughter Cholie is seventeen years old now. My foster parents adopted her, and she has their last name. My daughter and I have a good relationship, but she bonded with my foster mom much more than with me. We do some holidays together. She was born in the USA, and it's all she's ever known. I didn't know how to be a mother when I was so young, and my foster parents took care of my daughter and me. I wouldn't have made it without them, and I'm thankful they've given my daughter a good life.

Now we also have a son and another daughter, and it's difficult to know they won't be able to meet their grandmother and great-grandmother. When things come up, such as Grandparents Day at school, it would be nice for them to be able to participate. My husband's family is in the Chicago area, so we don't see them much either.

I'm open to talking about the war and my parents with my daughter. She's a teenager now, but isn't interested in knowing more at this age. I've made it available if and when she changes her mind.

I attended Holland Christian High School, went on to Calvin College, majoring in international studies, and minoring in social work. Then I went to Grand Rapids Theological Seminary where I studied for a master's in ministry leadership.

Now I work for the American Bible Society Mission Trauma Healing program. I speak and train people to work with children who need trauma healing. Children can experience trauma even while still in the womb. While I was growing up, people would often try to cheer me up, and said, "Everything's going to be okay." They try to make you happy because you're a child. When your parents disappear in a war, or playmates are killed, it's traumatic. I believe in coming right out and talking about it. Children should be surrounded by counseling to discuss how they're feeling.

I wish my mom could pass on knowledge and wisdom to me. She could sit with me and say things like, "Now you're going to have a family and create your own legacy. You will always be my daughter, but now you're going to be someone else's mother. You're studying social work, and I'm so proud of you." I'd love to hear those kinds of words from her. If I could, I'd like to hear how she felt when she was pregnant with me or stories about my childhood.

I know my mother loved the Lord Jesus, and I look forward to passing the Christian faith on to my children. I have very little memory of my mom, but since she was a kind person, I try to emulate that. She would want me to love the Lord and love others.

The only possession I have from my mom is a necklace made of bone in the shape of a cross, which she used to wear. When we were running from the village, my mom gave it to my uncle to give to me.

When people think of war, they don't tend to consider the suffering of women and children. The defenseless and weak are victims. Most people get out of the country fast or think of a way to avoid obstacles, but there are so many women and children who get left behind in trouble. That breaks my heart. It's why I have this profession now. My job enables me to speak to large groups, but I also mentor a few girls on the side here and there if they make special requests. I use Skype, phone, or Bible studies. I want them to know they're normal if they are afraid or feel like God abandoned them. We often focus on the book of Psalms, which many times talks about, "Why God, why me?" We encourage the girls by showing them a healthy way to grieve their losses and celebrate when healing comes.

I can relate somewhat to Jesus Christ's suffering on earth, because He didn't do anything wrong, but was traumatized and suffered more than anyone. My heart is completely His, but sometimes life goes in never ending circles of pain. At times I sob and ask God, "Why me?" At those times I know the Holy Spirit is my comforter.

If I could talk to a woman who has lost their mother, I'd say, "I feel you. Grieving well is important so give yourself time and plenty of space. I think it's healthy to express grief, but don't stay there. If you can remember any good times, celebrate them."

Bible verses:

*Above all else, guard your heart, for everything you do flows from it.* Proverbs 4:23

*He has shown you, O mortal, what is good. And what does the LORD require of you? To act justly and to love mercy and to walk humbly with your God.*

Micah 6:8

# TWO SISTERS GOT THROUGH IT TOGETHER

# Chapter 13

## One Little Rose

## With Carla

*Carla was almost thirty-one at the time of the interview. She is two years younger than her sister Lisa, who is featured in Chapter 14. Her mom, Linda, was forty at the time of her death on August 11, 1998, when Carla was thirteen years old.*

My mom died at the age of forty, which seems scary since that's less than ten years older than I am now. She was diagnosed with a form of acute leukemia, which is a cancer of the blood. She was given six months to live, but she made it one and a half years.

My mom had a lot of bruising and tiredness, but she was a busy mom and didn't come right out to tell her daughters, "I have bruising." After going to the doctor one day, my parents asked us to sit in the living room and told us her diagnosis. My sister Lisa and I were quiet and couldn't comprehend it.

The doctor wanted her to begin chemo immediately, but she refused, saying, "No, I'm going home to tell my girls first. We'll start tomorrow." The whirlwind began the very next day. She had to have very long hospital stays. We accompanied my dad to Butterworth in Grand Rapids to see her after school or in the summer because we were quite young. We wanted to see her, and I'm sure she wanted to see us.

Maybe she had to stay there because they didn't have cancer centers back then, or because her immune system was so weak. I'm not sure. But it became normal to go to the hospital. We weren't crying all the time. It was just routine to go along to visit her. She had a little couch in her room where we'd sometimes watch TV or do homework.

My mom had a lot of chemo, bone marrow tests, and ports and wires were attached to her. She never complained in front of us, even though I know it was awful. At first, I thought she was just sick and would get better. She said she was going to fight cancer. Sometimes the results after tests and chemo were good and sometimes bad. They tried some experimental things, but finally it came to a point where there wasn't anything else to do, and we decided to make the most of our time together. Sometimes she even rallied to play miniature golf or go shopping with us.

We were raised in the church, which was right across the street. The only reason you could get out of going to church was if you were down in bed with chickenpox or something. My mom was able to attend when I made profession of my faith in church when I was thirteen years old. She was such a huge influence on me; she lived her faith. She had her Bible at her side at all times. It was so marked up by the end of her life. She'd often say, "God's got a plan, God's will be done. I know where I'm going."

During my mom's illness, everyone at school knew our mom was sick, but they didn't fully understand. My dad checked up on us, asking how we were. He tried, but I often shut down and refused to talk personally with him. My sister and I had to do laundry, cleaning, ironing, and cooking. My dad was understandably more focused on the bills, his work, the yard, and the doctor appointments.

One time when I was home alone with my mom, all of a sudden, she ran to the bathroom to vomit. I peeked in and asked, "Mom, are you okay? Do you want me to call Dad?"

She said, "No, I'm fine, just get me some Sprite." I never saw my mom vomit, and I felt helpless and frightened. That was a while before her death, and I realized it was very serious, and thought, *She isn't going to make it, and she isn't going to get better.* Later on, we had hospice come in every week to help.

A few days before she died, my dad said she wasn't doing well, and we should tell her goodbye. He coached us on what to say. I said, "It's okay, Mom, you can go to heaven." She was in a hospital bed in the living room of our house. I didn't want to say goodbye to her. I didn't want her to give up. I didn't want her to go. I wondered why I had to say, "It's okay to go." Now I understand that chronically ill people need that sometimes.

As a mother of two teenage girls, everything must have been very traumatic for her. As a mother now myself, I get that. She became unconscious for her last few days. My aunt and uncle took my sister and me out to the beach campground. I think they wanted us to get away. During a meal, my uncle received a call on his car phone from my dad that my mom had just passed away, and they drove us back home. Lots of relatives were already in the house. There was my dead mother lying in the living room. It was uncomfortable having so many people around. I didn't feel like I could cry. I escaped upstairs to my bedroom when I could.

The funeral visitations were a marathon. We had two long sessions in one day. I didn't cry much there because I was already cried out. I went through the motions to answer people when they commented to me but felt numb. I agreed: "Yes, she's in heaven. Yes, she was a wonderful person. Thank you for your sympathies." The people all knew me, but being so young, I didn't know a lot of their names. Friends my age also came through.

Our youth pastor's wife, who was a doctor, often visited my mom in the hospital. When they came through the visitation, he brought a rose to my sister and me. I thought, *They're here for me. I know them.* They weren't just there for my dad. I don't think he realized how much that one little rose meant to us.

The funeral was called a celebration of her life. I cried during the whole service. We sang some old but powerful songs, "Great is Thy Faithfulness," and "Blessed Be the Name of the Lord." The pastor used my mom's own Bible in the service to talk about verses she loved.

After going to the gravesite for her burial, we came back to the church and did the whole lunch thing. I thought, *Just pull yourself together. Forget about it for a while.* It was good to take a break from crying, and we were able to laugh too. It helped to have family around, and especially my sister Lisa. We had always gotten along pretty well, but this brought us even closer. I thought, *You're the only one who knows how much this stinks.*

Some people tried to help my sister and me before and after my mom's death. Our girlfriends and their moms had us over or took us shopping. A couple, who were best friends of the family, had us over or visited often. My aunt was always available for us, as were my mom's parents and my stepmom, who was then still a family friend. We had so much food coming in, I felt like I couldn't eat any more. People were very helpful and caring.

When I saw another girl yelling at her mom, I thought, *You don't know how lucky you are. You have your mom. Snap out of it! I don't have my mother.* Sometimes I had anger or depression. One time I kicked the door in the high school bathroom stall, I was so angry and ticked about life. I had regressed. Sometimes there's a trigger and something hits you. You wonder if you might need medications or something to get you through. Thankfully, each time the wave passed over again.

My dad married my stepmom about one and a half years after my mom passed away. The marriage was too soon for me at the time, but later I learned that Mom and Dad talked about it, and Mom had encouraged him to move on with her. It makes me regret some of my inner feelings at the time. They had all been friends for a long time, and her husband died several years before. It was uncomfortable and awkward at first, but we adjusted. It was kind of nice to have home-cooked meals and not have to do all the housework alone. After they married, we moved into her farmhouse, and we've all blended well over the years. After a few more years, my sister and I both went to college. Now I can't imagine not having her big family in my life.

I definitely can see how this affected the way that I mother. When my daughter was two, I still rocked her to sleep for naps and bedtime. It was a challenge to conceive; she was our miracle baby. Now we've also been blessed with our son! I worry I won't be there for my children. When I see a bruise, I panic, *Oh no! Do I need to go to the doctor?* Sometimes I try not to depend on others to care for my children, feeling guilty for asking because I want to do it all myself.

My daughter never knew my mom, but last year I took her to the gravesite for the first time and we laid some flowers. As I touched the gravestone, I said, "This is your grandma, and she's with Jesus in heaven."

She won't understand much until she's older, but I want to keep speaking about her. Sometimes we look at my mom's photographs too. My mom would be so proud to know that I fulfilled my lifetime dream of becoming a nurse, just like her. I really wanted to talk to her about our challenges with infertility. Although it was mild compared to others, it was very hard for me.

My stepmom is amazing and has done so much for me. Especially since being a mom now, I realize how much. My dad would have appreciated it if we called her mom but didn't force us. I'm respectful because she has taken us under her wings as total daughters. But we don't call her Mom. The word Mom is just reverent. She and my daughter have a true granddaughter-grandmother relationship.

If I could talk to my mom, I'd like to know what heaven is like. I'd ask her what she was thinking and feeling during her illness. Also, everyday things like, "The kids won't take a nap, what should I do? What do you think about this situation at work?" This is when I'm very thankful for a sister too. We kind of became mothers to each other.

When we were cleaning out my mom's closet after the funeral, my dad gave us a letter she wrote to each of us. I haven't read it in a while because it makes me cry, but it's so precious. She told me to stay close to God, watch over Dad, and go to my aunt or her best friend if I needed anything. It's so nice to see her handwriting. How do you sum that up, to be kind, compassionate, and have faith? I can't imagine writing a letter to my daughter, condensing it down to a couple pages to last her a lifetime.

The whole thing changes you, and it stinks sometimes. A blog post of a friend who lost her dad said, "It's a club you don't want to be a part of, but once you're in it, you're in it for life." You have to decide to have it change you for the better. On my mom's gravestone it says, "Thy Will Be Done." It's true, God has a plan, and we must trust it's all for good.

My mom touched so many lives. We recently returned to my childhood church after I was gone for sixteen years. We were welcomed, and many still tell me things like, "Your mom was so special." What do you say, "Thank you?" I don't know exactly how to respond, but it's nice to know she's remembered. I strive to be like my mom. I'd like to have people come up to my kids many years later and tell them things like that.

It gives me hope to know that she's healed and in heaven. I miss her, but I know I'll see her again. It's not the end! Every day I keep going because my husband and children need me.

I took care of my grandpa when he was old and valued that time before he died. It seemed like something I could do for him and also for my mom. Since she was a nurse, she would have helped him if she were alive. He wasn't my direct parent, yet I was the sandwich generation.

I don't fear death as much now. It would be nerve-wracking to get sick because I don't want to leave my husband and children. As a teenager or college student, there were some days I just would have preferred to get out of this crummy world. I thought I would like to go to heaven and meet Jesus and family members who've passed away. Not that I ever planned anything, but the feeling was there. I needed to decide to help others and not be down in the dumps.

If your mom has passed away, I'm sorry. Those of us who've gone through it are here for you. It will get easier, but there will be days you're not okay. Hopefully, you have your faith to lean on, and loved ones around you. You really have to decide to keep going and make things as positive as you can. Try to help others. I think I'm a better person after going through all this.

I didn't remember how young I was. It breaks my heart that I've forgotten a lot about her. Memories will continue to fade, and I wish I could remember all of the good things. God is faithful. He has a bigger plan and will help us through.

Bible verses:

*For I know the plans I have for you. . .* Jeremiah 29:11

"Your will be done," is on my mom's gravestone with some praying hands. There was a lot of praying going on through it all. It's a key component in bad situations.

*Therefore do not worry about tomorrow, for tomorrow will worry about itself. Each day has enough trouble of its own.* Matthew 6:34

With all the stress back then, and in my current daily life, I have to remember not to worry. God's got this.

*Pray continually, give thanks in all circumstances; for this is God's will for you in Christ Jesus.* 1 Thessalonians 5:17–18

Giving thanks in all circumstances is hard but we need to rejoice in all.

*Do not be anxious about anything, but in every situation, by prayer and petition, with thanksgiving, present your requests to God. And the peace of God which transcends all understanding, will guard your hearts and your minds in Christ Jesus.* Philippians 4:6–7

I still pray, "God just give me peace, through it all."

# Chapter 14

# Star Gazing

# With Lisa

*Lisa is two years older than her sister Carla, featured in Chapter 13. Lisa was thirty-three at the time of the interview. Her mom, Linda, died at the age of forty, when Lisa was fifteen years old.*

One day, as I was leaving for school, Mom stopped me in the kitchen and said, "Hey, Mom has to go to the doctor, haven't been feeling good. We're going to see what's going on." That's when they began doctoring and found her cancer. It was called acute lymphatic cancer of the blood.

It was a year and a half from the diagnosis to her death. During my freshman year in high school, I dealt with her illness. She died just before my sophomore year. When I went back to school that fall, I was the girl whose mom died.

She always had Christian radio on, *Focus on the Family*, and those types of programs. She was so full of faith, very involved in church, Bible studies, and women's groups. We all went to church twice on Sundays and Wednesday nights without question. It was very convenient, since we lived in the red brick house right across the street from our church.

My mom was such a busy woman, worked in the kitchen, in her garden, and tended the flowers outside. We helped her cook and clean. We took family walks and picked vegetables in the garden. I was on the softball team in high school, and she came to see me play even when she was sick.

My mom would often talk about her faith, and when she got sick, she dug into her Bible even more. She memorized verses too. I took her Bible along today, which is kept in her hope chest, now in my home along with many of my mom's possessions. I hadn't looked in it for a long time.

I was basically a Christian all my life, always in Sunday school, vacation Bible school, and camp. I definitely had anger toward God for her sickness and death. I had moments of wrestling with Him but stayed with the faith. It was amazing that I didn't walk away. I still prayed, went to youth group and everything but had a rebellious attitude toward God.

At age thirteen, I made a profession of faith in church before she became ill. I took it seriously, but I had a childlike faith. I have a picture of my mom and me together on that day.

When she was sick, we rode along with my dad to see my mom in the hospital many times. We sat there on the couch in her room, watching TV or doing our homework. People sent many cards, and she put them up on the walls with poster putty. She didn't look good, and I think she was in pain but tried to hide it. She really didn't want her girls to see something that would scare them.

Throughout my mom's illness, I was angry about it. I clammed up with my parents and wanted to stay in my own little world. My mom tried to talk to me, but I gave one-word answers or shrugged my shoulders. I was all about doing anything I could to feel normal again.

At one point, I went into autopilot mode and thought, *Okay, this is the new normal. We just have to figure this out.* My dad did the best he could, and Carla and I stuck together. We were always close, but this brought us much closer. My dad tried to talk to us and keep the lines of communication open. He often cooked, although we had an abundance of food coming in from family and church friends.

Something I did often while growing up was to go outside in the parking lot next to our house and lay down to look at the sky. One night, towards the end, just before she became really sick, I went out there. It was my alone time with God, and I was finally able to voice the words, "You can take her now. She's been through enough." I finally came to terms with it.

That was a big thing for me. I gazed at all the stars and cried and prayed to God.

After being in the hospital for rounds of chemo and radiation, she was under hospice care at home in a hospital bed in the living room the last couple weeks, where they simply tried to control her pain.

A couple days before her passing, we came home from camping to visit with our parents. I think everyone knew it was getting close to the time. My mom was sentimental and weepy, and I was thinking, Stop being so emotional. As we sat around and talked, I felt like, *Let's get back to camping.* When it was time to leave, my mom cried and said, "Goodbye, I love you." For whatever reason, I could only say, "I'll see you later." I don't think I knew she was that close to death. My dad tried to be intentional to call us back for the afternoon, but wanted to shield us from the pain of actually seeing her moment of death.

That was the last time I saw her, and I wasn't warm towards her. That's something I have to deal with now. I often gave her the cold shoulder, as she was hard to look at. She had a butch haircut after losing all her hair, various wigs, wore baseball caps, and her fingernails were gross and had band-aids on them. Earlier on, we tried to go shopping at the mall, with Mom in a wheelchair. I was at the age that I wanted to fit in, and I definitely was not fitting in.

On the day my mom died, we were still camping near the beach with our aunt and uncle. I think my dad wanted to instill a sense of normalcy for us and get us out of the house. My uncle received a phone call from my dad, and I just knew, *Okay, this is it.* Anger boiled in me. I went into the camper and chucked my clothes into a suitcase. I think her body was already gone when we arrived back home. My dad was at the door. He hugged us, and we cried. The rest of that day I retreated up to my bedroom.

At the visitation, the tradition was to stand in a row while people waited in line to walk past you. It was expected that we greet every person. I stood by my dad, and there were so many friends, relatives, and church people. It was awkward for me because it was an open casket, and she had the sick, makeup-caked face. It all seemed so abnormal. A group of my friends came through.

Our pastor and our youth pastor led the funeral service. I was in such a daze and still very angry. I think I've finally worked through most of that. My husband encouraged me to go to counseling eight years later. I'm glad I went because it gave me some closure. I think it was offered to my sister and me by hospice right away, but I brushed it off and said I was fine. It's too bad that counseling has such a bad stigma to it. I think it's good for anyone.

I have some regret about not spending those last days or moments with her. Being a typical fifteen-year-old, I had a bad attitude at the last meeting with her and earlier on too. I think I came off as very cold and uncaring and was often mean and selfish. It was my mom! Now, being a mom myself, I look back and understand I must have hurt her.

We have a young daughter and a son. I'm really glad I had a girl first. If we had a boy first, it would have been fantastic. I love having a boy now too! But I think to have a daughter healed a mother-daughter relationship that got broken off. I know how my mother mothered me, being a girl, and now I can take my best memories and transport it to her. I do things with her that my mom did with me, such as going to feed ducks.

I give my kids the best things, probably to a fault. Whatever the latest things are, I want to get them for my kids. On the flip side of that, I don't know if it's just a normal mother thing, but I have high anxiety about them getting sick. Not necessarily terminal illness but general sicknesses and flu. I realize I'm borderline overprotective, and am the first to admit it. I'm a mother hen.

I plan to make it a tradition to go to my mom's gravesite on the anniversary of her passing, to bring a flower and talk about my mom with my daughter. I say, "Remember Grandma Linda, she's the one who's in heaven with Jesus? She was important to me." Of course, she didn't know her, but I want her to make the connection who my mom was. I explain that the Grandma she knows isn't my mom. She'll understand as time goes by.

My dad married my stepmom after a little over a year. It was too soon for me and hard at first. Dad said Mom had pointed him in her direction, and Mom and Dad had talked about it, as they were all friends. Mom had asked him to mourn for a year. There were big adjustments for all of us.

My stepmom didn't do anything to cause me not to jump in one hundred percent. She never overstepped her boundaries, was kind, gentle, and understanding. It would have been hard for anyone to step into that position and they would have gotten the same reaction from me. It was a huge change to move into her farmhouse. In some ways, it was a pleasant change, as Carla and I had our own bedrooms, because her children were mostly out of the house. Thinking back, I know I was often unkind, which wasn't fair to anyone. Soon I turned sixteen and got my driver's license. I was only there a couple years, then lived on campus at college, and married soon after graduation.

My sister and I were somewhat of mentors for each other and very close friends. We had to grow up fast. We understood each other because we went through something so life-changing, and that put us on the same level even though she was two years younger. We also had aunts and friends who kept tabs on us and often helped us out.

Of course, there are times when I wished my mom could have been there, like the obvious big ones. But probably more so, the random weird days, crummy days when I am down. I would ask her, "Is this normal, Mom? Am I going off the deep end? This is hard with the baby; did this happen to you?" Breast-feeding questions, you know. Carla and I talk about all these things.

Sometimes I really wish I could talk to my mom about the whole parenting thing. Because she didn't journal much, I find myself wanting to know her thoughts. I'm always looking on other's blogs, talking to friends, taking pieces from what others have learned. I'm looking for clues from other moms on how to parent well. Maybe I could parent better if I had her advice, or she could say, "Learn from my mistakes. You don't have to worry about that." Now I would like to know the messy parts too, like, "How much pain were you in?" The parts I didn't want to hear then, I want to know now.

On the holidays, I think of my mom, but it's such a busy time. I always find the card I would have gotten for my mom. Not on purpose, but I always see it and think that would have been the one. I have a love of baking from my mom. Recently, I was on a mission to find her blueberry muffin recipe and found it from my dad's sister. We made memories on some great family vacations, like Disney World, Mackinaw Island, Sault Ste. Marie, and Shipshewana.

I have some of my mom's possessions, such as this Bible. Many things were in the hope chest. There was a letter from my dad to her, written about us girls on Mother's Day. There's also a letter to me from mom. I keep it in a frame with her picture. Her Bible is full of markings and notes. We gave her this Bible toward the end when she was sick. My mom wrote on a piece of paper the passages of Proverbs 3:5–6 and Psalm 46:10. She wrote a short story for someone to read at her funeral.

My mom taught me to stick with things, keep going, and don't lose sight of who's in control. She always tried to keep a positive attitude even when she was sick in the hospital or at home. It was so clear to her that God had a plan.

My greatest hope is the forever home in heaven when we're done with this life down here on earth. Sometimes I wish it would come sooner rather than later, and other days it feels like life here on earth is good. I try to live a life that serves Christ, and I'm looking forward to seeing my mom again.

I empathize with girls who have lost their mother. Obviously, I've been there. I try to keep an eye out for those trying to hide and secretly going through it like I did as a teenager. Maybe I've helped others without even knowing it.

Life can go on after a traumatic death. It takes time, and you grow from it. It's okay to miss them and be sad about it. It's also okay to have a good time occasionally. I've only gotten to this point recently, that I think death is exciting in a way. I've matured through the grieving process and have grown in my faith. My grandfather just passed away, and now I can think, *He's not suffering anymore! He got to hug his daughter who he hasn't seen in fifteen years.* There's so much more in heaven!

It's extremely hard to lose your mother. It gets a little easier with time. Your mom wouldn't want you to stay in one place. Remember the special moments and enjoy them. Hard times have a way of letting you look at life in a better way.

It was good to talk about this and think about my mom again because it's part of who I am. God's been faithful and has given so many blessings over the years. It's always good to refresh the memories.

Bible Verses:

*He will wipe every tear from their eyes. There will be no more death or mourning or crying or pain, for the old order of things has passed away.* Revelation 21:4

*Trust in the LORD with all your heart and lean not on your own understanding.* Proverbs 3:5

*Cast all your anxiety on him because he cares for you.* 1 Peter 5:7

In the commentary of my Bible, it describes Isaiah 38, by explaining that Hezekiah did not give up praying when he had a fatal disease, and he was granted fifteen more years of life. God changes events because of prayer. I highlighted that, because I wanted more years with my mom, but that wasn't in God's plan right now.

# FOUR SISTERS, TWO MOMS' DEATHS

# Chapter 15

## Meet Me Over in Glory Land

## With Marilyn Tinklenberg

*This family called their moms by first, second, and third, instead of "step." Marilyn was five years old when her biological mom, Tena, died, in 1947, at the age of twenty-seven. Marilyn was twenty-two when her second mom, Bertha, died at the age of forty-one, in 1964. On the date of this interview, Marilyn was seventy-three years old.*

My mom, Tena, died when she was only twenty-seven years old, on February 5, 1947. I was five years old, and my sister was two years younger. I only have a few remembrances of my mom. She had been sick for months before they finally did surgery. She couldn't eat, but she drank Welch's grape juice a great deal.

I was very young, so I don't remember the actual moment of her death. My dad didn't take us to the funeral. I remember the day; the neighbor lady came to take care of my sister and me. She brought a meal and stayed with us while my dad and other family members went to the funeral. In those days, usually young children were not taken to funerals, but I know her body was in our home for some days before the funeral, which was a common practice in those days. My dad took us to the living room to see her in the coffin. I realized she was dead, and vividly remember my little sister Carol saying she was sleeping.

My mom had been sick with terrible attacks of pain. Back then, they didn't have the means to figure it out, such as ultrasounds. She tried eliminating certain foods from her diet, but nothing helped. The surgery performed to remove her gall bladder was a failure, so poison apparently spread all through her body. They tried a second surgery some days later while she was still in the hospital, but the doctors were baffled. She was getting sicker.

My dad took us to visit my mom at the hospital. Children were usually not allowed, but they let us in because I think they knew she was dying. My Aunt Henrietta took care of us a lot during that time, and she gave me a little church purse, which I showed to my mom. They didn't do autopsies then either. I wish I could ask my dad more about it, but he's gone now too. We were told she went to heaven and she was in a better place. At first, my dad didn't talk about it at all. Years later we did, but I don't know many details.

Ironically, I had gall bladder problems at the same age as my mom did. The hospitals were so busy then, and unless it was an emergency, they didn't do surgeries. I had to wait a month before I had surgery. My dad was very concerned about me, because it made him relive it all again. My surgery and health turned out fine.

Aunt Henrietta gave me a plaque after my mom died, which said, "My loving mother, she is gone, she asked us all to follow on, she said work for Jesus while you can, and meet me over in glory land."

A special memento we have of my mom is a piece of her hair. At one time, she had a large amount cut off, and they saved a strand about ten inches long. She had coarse, thick hair, which they wrapped in paper and put it in a tiny box. It's still in my cedar chest today, along with a saved section of her wedding dress and a baby book she made for me.

My mom's passing was so hard on all of us. One time I saw my dad leaning over the barn door, just sobbing. The door was in halves, the top open to circulate air, and bottom half stayed shut to keep the cows in. It was really clear in my mind that he was crying, even though I was only five years old.

Neighbor ladies would often bring dinner and took care of us girls. We had a hired housekeeper for a while, and several relatives helped out. A year and a half after my mom died, my dad married Bertha, in 1948, when

I was six years old. She was the mom who raised me the most. She was my second mom. My dad insisted that we called her mom, and it became natural after a while. Now, when we talk amongst us sisters, we say, "first mom, second mom, third mom," so we know who we're talking about. For years, on Memorial Day, we went out as a family to place pansies on my first mom's grave, because she loved them. My dad, Bertha, and all of us kids went to honor her.

My mom Bertha made us feel very loved even though we weren't her biological daughters. Sometimes Carol and I thought her kids were favored, but it wasn't true. Later you realize, they also worked on the farm and in the house.

I have a lot of memories of my second mom, Bertha. She was my mom from age six to twenty-two. She taught me how to sew, and I still sew a great deal today. It's my livelihood and gives me purpose and fun. She was a great mother to us, physically and spiritually. She was a strong Christian mother, and I give her most of the credit for my beliefs and faith. When she helped us with our catechism lessons, she would explain the answers we didn't understand. It was evident from everyday living and talk that she had a very strong faith.

When we heard about my mom Bertha's death, my husband and I were eating dinner at my Aunt Martha and Uncle Gordon's house in West Michigan. We received the call and left the next day for Minnesota. She died very unexpectedly of a heart problem while she was home with my dad and the kids. It was probably a heart defect that runs in her family, but at that time, it was inconclusive as to the reason she died.

My kids haven't asked much about my first mom, Tena, because they never knew any different. My third child wasn't even born when my second mom, Bertha, died. My oldest, Dave, went along to mom Bertha's funeral when he was two years old. After my dad married Opal, my third mom, she was the grandma all three of our kids grew to know and love.

I know both my first and second moms were sure of their salvation, so I look forward to seeing them again in heaven. It all boils down to my faith in God. If someone doesn't have that, I don't know how they can go on. He is in control, and we don't know why things like this happen, but we believe God has a larger plan and purpose.

I have tried to help my sisters over the years, but we lived far away. It was very hard to leave my younger sisters after my mom Bertha's funeral. I wished I could have stayed to take care of them, but I had two small children and my husband was attending seminary in Michigan. Lots of tears were shed. Hopefully, I've helped them in our talks and letters over the years.

The death of both of my moms made me realize you don't have to be old to die. When you're a teenager, you think you're going to keep living on until you're old. My mom was only twenty-seven, and my second mom was only forty-one, which is still young. It all made me realize you should always be prepared.

It's not easy to lose a mom. Remember the good times and keep trusting in the Lord. He will give you the comfort and strength you need to get through bad times.

We all adjusted to our changes over the years and got along with one another, by the grace of God. It was a hard childhood in some ways, but I was blessed with three wonderful moms.

Bible Verses:

*I will never leave you nor forsake you.* Joshua 1:5

My parents taught me this verse from Joshua when I was quite young. It has often come to mind throughout my life.

*The LORD is a refuge for the oppressed, a stronghold in times of trouble. Those who know your name trust in you, for you, LORD, have never forsaken those who seek you.* Psalm 9:9–10

# Chapter 16
# Held by the Everlasting Arms
# With Carol Teske

*Carol was seventy-one years old at the time of the interview. Her mom, Tena, died at twenty-seven years old, in 1947, when Carol was two and a half years old. Her second mom, Bertha, died in 1964, at the age of forty-one. At that time, Carol was nineteen years old.*

I am certain of my mom's Christian faith because of the way I was raised. My parents were strong believers. I always knew about Jesus, from a very young age, raised to trust in God and have faith. Credit goes to my parents for teaching me about the love of God.

Since I was so young, I don't know much about the day of her death. The only memory I have of my mother was seeing her in the casket. Back then, they placed the body in the home for a few days. My dad lifted me up to see her lying there in her blue dress. My sister Marilyn told me that I said, "She's sleeping." You don't remember much from two and a half years old, but a couple things are very clear in my mind. I don't have memories of doing activities with my mom because she was ill for a long time before she died, with gall bladder problems. She went in for surgery and had complications. Later they tried a second surgery, but she died about a month later.

After my mom passed away, we had a hired woman, Etta, do some household chores. Also, Aunt Henrietta, my dad's youngest sister, lived with us to take care of my sister and me for a time.

A few of my mom's belongings were in the house as I was growing up. We had a large lock of my mom's hair wrapped in tissue paper in a little box, scraps of her wedding dress, some pictures, and a few pieces of jewelry. It was nice to have her hair to give me an idea of what color it was. Her wedding dress was a deep rose color, not white, which was common then.

There are two pictures of her holding me when I was around ten months old, which are the only baby pictures of me that have been found. My mom was often sick when I was young, and they were busy farmers. There's nothing more I can say about my biological mom. I was just too young to know much.

My dad married Bertha in 1948, when I was four. Bertha lived in Michigan, and through relatives, my dad began writing letters to her. I remember driving from Minnesota to Michigan to visit Bertha. They didn't even make phone calls, because long-distance calls were very expensive.

Bertha was the one who raised me through my childhood and teens, from age four to nineteen. As far as relationships, I was often in my own little world, somewhat of an introvert. I think I blocked things out because I remember very few details. The hurt of losing people made me set up some walls. I don't think I was consciously thinking people would die. Taking long walks, curling up in a tree and reading for hours, ignoring what was going on and not getting too involved in things were my preference when I was around ten or eleven. I participated in family activities, but I enjoyed being by myself. When I got married, I used to say it was because my husband was in the military. You make close friends and then have to say goodbye when you move, so I tended to put up boundaries to prevent building close relationships.

Bertha was a wonderful mom. I am amazed by what she went through, marrying someone with two little kids, moving out in the country to do work on a farm, into a house with no plumbing. She had to be a saint. When I was disciplined, I thought at times, *You're not my real mom.* How hurtful it would have been if I had said it out loud, and I hope I never did. She did the day-to-day work, made sure we knew our catechism lessons, made meals, and took excellent loving care of all of us.

After a car accident my folks had, she had a blood clot or something in her ankle, and was in bed. Whether the clot moved, or if it was because of the heart problem which runs in the family, we're not sure. She suddenly sat up in bed and said, "Harry!" That was it. She died. What a shock for my younger sisters who were right there when it happened.

The pastor from the Holland, Minnesota church came to my college to get me when my mom passed away. I was nineteen years old. No one even called me first. He found me and drove me home. I was attending nursing school in Sioux Falls, about one hour away from home.

One thing is clear. When I arrived home, my little brother Frank, who was around six years old, ran to me and hugged me. It was as if he thought, *Oh, it's so chaotic here, and here's someone I know! Someone who can pay attention to me.* It's interesting how I tend to remember things from a very young age, but not very much from when I was older. I don't remember anything about the visitations or funeral.

A week after the funeral, I had to go right back to nursing school. That created guilt feelings for a long time because my younger sisters, Nancy, and Faith, were really burdened with a lot of work. They were going to school, making meals, taking care of the house, and working on the farm with my dad.

When Bertha died, I rebelled somewhat. It was another person in my life who died. I thought maybe if I went far away it would help. For some time, I drifted away from God. I went out West, met and married Clay, my military man, did my own thing, and started a brand-new life. I believed in God, but was busy with many moves and didn't think I needed God to direct my steps every day. When we had our child, Lisa, we got back into church, and I think that's when I finally began to grow deeper in my faith. I came home yearly, wrote letters, and remained close with family, but I was quite independent. My walk with God has grown closer in the second half of my life.

My dad married Opal a few months after Clay and I got married. Dad and Opal came down to visit us in New Mexico, while on their honeymoon. She is the only grandma my daughter Lisa ever knew and they're very special to one another.

I'm sure we will be one joyous family in heaven one day. Maybe all the relationships won't matter, but we'll know each other, we won't have regrets about what happened in the past, and it will be glorious. I have faith that all things happen for a reason. We certainly can't sort those things out now. In the end, there will be happiness and joy if we just believe. I guess from early on I knew life is very uncertain, and it changes all the time. I'm not at all afraid of death, because I was raised in faith and love of God.

I have empathy and understanding, having lost two moms. If you're still having heartache and problems with a hole in your life, take it to God. His love will help you through.

Bible Verse:

*The eternal God is your refuge, and underneath are the everlasting arms.* Deuteronomy 33:27

I love that His arms are always beneath me to support and hold me.

## Chapter 17

## Pass the Blessing On

## With Nancy Maas

*Nancy was sixty-six at the time of the interview. Her mom, Bertha, was forty-one at her death, on March 1, 1964, when Nancy was fourteen years old.*

At the time of my mom's death, I was right there. Mom and Dad had been in a car accident a couple weeks before, and she had a badly sprained ankle. So, she relaxed in bed, while the rest of us went to an afternoon church service. As we changed our clothes after church, my dad hollered for us. She had been reclining against the pillows and suddenly sat up and took a gasping breath. Her heart probably went into a bad rhythm. She fell back and couldn't breathe.

I came to the doorway; my dad began crying. He said, "Mom is going to die." He asked me to call the doctor. You had to go to the other room to the phone on the wall. We all just stood around crying. He told me a second time to call the doctor.

I said to him, "You can call." So, my dad asked me to stay next to my mom while he went to call the doctor. When my dad returned, I said to him, "When I shook her shoulders, she breathed a little bit."

It seems so silly that I said that. I always felt bad that I should have made the phone call because dad probably wanted to stay with her. But when you're fourteen, you're not used to calling doctors and saying your mom is dying. My dad cried out to God, saying, "Oh God, not again." He had already lost one wife at this point. I think it's good that he could express himself because so often people didn't do that, especially in those days.

The doctor came over to pronounce her dead. Many people came over, and we had to feed them all coffee and snacks. Many people said to me, "Oh, you've lost your mother." At the time, you don't have any idea how sad it is to lose your mother. You're just trying to get through it. Of course, we were sad, but we didn't know how hard it would be through the years.

It was obvious that my mom had a strong faith. We read the Bible three times a day after meals, we went to church, we saw her reading her Bible and devotionals. I think most people didn't talk openly about their faith in those days, but you knew she had the joy of the Lord and was such a gentle and kind person. Music was an important part of her life and faith. On Sunday nights, we would all gather around the piano. She played, and we all sang. She had played the viola in the Holland Christian High School orchestra, but she didn't own one to play. My mom taught me a great deal without using words. She modeled gentleness. I don't remember ever hearing her yell.

I had a solid faith since I was young. There was never a time I didn't know about Jesus; He was always a huge part of our family. I was a serious-minded child, and when I was in about second grade, we had bunk beds in the little room off our kitchen. I tried to go to sleep, but I was troubled and crying. My dad came in and asked me what was wrong. I told him I was afraid because I wasn't sure if I was going to heaven. My dad prayed with me, asking the Lord to give me the assurance of knowing that I was a Christian. I could always look back and know that was the day my dad prayed the salvation prayer with me. I knew there was a heaven and a hell, and I was going to heaven.

The visitation and funeral aren't clear. For years, in my mind, I saw her in the coffin in her blue dress and remembered very few living memories of her. I know I cried hard at the gravesite, because it seemed so final when they put her into the ground. When we were leaving the cemetery, my high school principal came to speak to me. Of course, as a teen, I was embarrassed that I was crying, but over the years I've been so touched that he came.

Having a close relationship with my dad and sisters helped a great deal. My sisters, Faith, and Joanne, and I went through everything together and helped one another survive. You just do the next thing. When I look back now, my dad's faith and positive attitude, and also our circle of supporters in our little country church and school, made it possible to persevere.

My dad didn't want me to help in the barn milking cows anymore after my mom died, but wanted me to concentrate on the cooking and cleaning. He didn't remarry until about three years later. One time when I was a teenager, I felt inadequate when a group of ladies from church came over to do spring cleaning. I thought we were doing a decent job and felt humiliated by this. The people were kind and meant well, but in high school, you're trying to figure out who you are. When people want to help all the time, you feel like you must not be doing a good enough job.

I have many fond memories of working with my mom in the kitchen. She taught me how to can, bake, cook, and clean. When she died, I already knew how to do all the necessary things in the kitchen. She gave me piano lessons. I have a vivid memory of putting rollers in her hair the night before she died. I can't believe she was only forty-one when she died; she seemed so much older, because I was only fourteen. When I turned forty-one, it hit me how young she really was.

My mom sat at night and wrote letters and postcards, especially to her sister Martha. Things were cleared out of our small farmhouse over the years, and I'm not sure what happened to the letters she received. I also have some photographs of my childhood, but not many material items.

Of course, I always think about my mom's birth date and death date. After a few years, we couldn't talk about our mom much because we had a stepmom, and my dad insisted that we call her Mom. Faith and I had been in charge for three years, and my dad wanted us to back off in the kitchen. We liked Opal as a person, but it was a forced thing at first. I thought we had been moving along nicely, but I didn't have any understanding of the depth of loneliness my dad must have had. It was hard, but we all blended together.

When I disciplined my kids, I wondered if I had been a stubborn teenager. Being a mom yourself, you wish you had your mom to talk to. I always marveled at how she did it. She must have loved my dad so much, to leave the city, put aside her musical connections and a job in town, to move out on a forsaken farm with an outhouse and no running water. When she first married my dad, she also took care of two little stepdaughters.

After my mom died, I took life much more seriously because I began to realize that life is short. My constant prayer has been that I would get to raise my own children, to live long enough so they won't be motherless like I was. God really answered that prayer. I wanted to live longer for my kids and my sister Joanne's kids. She died when her boys were very young, and I did whatever I could to help them and their dad.

My kids never knew my mom. Their only grandma was Opal, my stepmom. They didn't experience the feeling of loss that I had, and she has been a wonderful grandmother to them.

There are two levels of hope I have. One is the spiritual level—that we will all be in heaven together and see one another there, and things will be perfect again. As far as changing the world, at the physical level, I hope our family can be in a position to get rid of the heart defect. Maybe in my grandkids' generation, it will be eradicated by wearing a chip or another great invention, and defibrillators won't be needed.

I facilitate a group at my church called "Grief Share," which is a part of a national organization, to help people deal with the death of a loved one. They have a wonderful biblical perspective on processing your grief. When going through the grief process, it's important to know other people have similar thoughts and feelings. Otherwise you feel like you're going crazy. I went through the program the first time soon after my husband, Wally, died. After two years, I became a group facilitator. It helps me to have God's perspective on things because I don't want to be a bitter old lady!

When people are grieving, I've tried to come alongside them. As a teenager, working in Grand Rapids, I stayed overnight with my nearby cousin, Eloise. It was only a couple months after her mom, my mom's sister, Aunt Martha, had died. You know how sometimes it's easier as a teenager to talk when you don't have to look a person in the eye. In the darkness, we could relate and talked and cried far into the night.

As I tell my story, I realize how deeply I must have been affected by my mom's death because well over fifty years later, I still cry. I'm more sensitive and aware that life is short, reminding me to value relationships. I'm much quicker to tell people how much I care about them because you don't know when you're going to lose them. Often, we wait until people die to say nice things about them and aren't kind while they're here. I think we should give others a blessing, and they can pass the blessing on to the next person.

If you've lost your mother, cherish the relationships you do have. If you're a mom, be the best mom you can. Pass on some of the character traits and values your mom had. Be aware, because some traits, good or bad, you pass on without even knowing it. I realized that life is not always what we planned, but somehow God's purposes are carried through.

Bible Verses:

*The LORD is my shepherd, I lack nothing. He makes me lie down in green pastures, he leads me beside quiet waters, he refreshes my soul. He guides me along the right paths for his name's sake. Even though I walk through the darkest valley, I will fear no evil, for you are with me; your rod and your staff, they comfort me. You prepare a table before me in the presence of my enemies. You anoint my head with oil; my cup overflows. Surely your goodness and love will follow me all the days of my life, and I will dwell in the house of the LORD forever.* Psalm 23

In high school, I went to Psalm 23 for strength. Memorizing it made it come alive for me. As an adult, I have a few verses that are my current favorites, which give me comfort and strength and remind me that I matter to God.

*But those who hope in the LORD will renew their strength. They will soar on wings like eagles; they will run and not grow weary; they will walk and not be faint.* Isaiah 40:31

*The eternal God is your refuge, and underneath are the everlasting arms.* Deuteronomy 33:27

*The LORD your God is with you, the Mighty Warrior who saves. He will take great delight in you; in his love he will no longer rebuke you, but will rejoice over you with singing.* Zephaniah 3:17

I love to think about what it sounds like when the Lord rejoices over us with singing! Can you imagine?

Myrna Folkert

## Chapter 18

## Longing to See

## With Faith VanArendonk

*Faith was sixty-five years old at the time of the interview. Her mom, Bertha, died at the age of forty-one years old, on March 1, 1964, when Faith was thirteen years old.*

My mom occasionally traveled to the Mayo Clinic in Rochester, because she had some kind of heart problem. As a little girl, I didn't know what it was all about, but it was most likely the heart defect which runs in our family line.

My parents had been in a car accident, which left my mom with some injuries. She hadn't gone to church with the rest of us because she was having back and ankle problems. When we arrived home one Sunday afternoon after the church service, she was sitting up, reading in bed. I talked to her very briefly before going to my bedroom to change clothes. I heard my dad yell, "Mom!" When I ran back to their bedroom, it looked like she was having a heart attack. My dad massaged her heart, attempting to revive her, but nothing seemed to help. She died right there in front of us. Later, my sisters and I sat in the front room, stunned. Soon relatives and neighbors arrived. Funeral home attendants came to take my mom's body out of the bedroom to a hearse.

At the time, they called my mom's death a heart attack. She had been going to the Mayo Clinic for appointments, but they were still trying to get to the bottom of it to figure out what it was and how to treat it. In later years, my cousin Helen studied the inherited Long QT syndrome, which helped shed light on the problem for many of my extended relatives.

Occasionally when I was growing up, my mom's sister Martha came out to our farm. She and my mom laughed and talked in the kitchen together. They must have really missed each other when my mom left Michigan to come out to Minnesota, and constantly wrote letters back and forth. My mom often sat late at night, writing letters and postcards. She often played the piano, and we'd all sing together. She gave us lessons, but my sisters were much more musical and dedicated than I was. When she started giving lessons to Nancy, I knew my turn was coming up, so I'd go outside to hop on the tractor with my dad. I loved being outside. My mom also played the viola in the orchestra during high school when she was growing up in Holland, Michigan, although she didn't own one. She also loved to play her classical music records in the house. There was usually some sort of music going on.

She included us in the cooking and baking, allowing us to scrape the batter out of the bowls. I'm thankful she taught me cooking skills. At various times, I'd sit on her bed and chitchat with her about anything. She was a good listener. As I got older, I wondered what it was like for her to move way out in the country on a farm when she married my dad. She grew up as a city girl and went to a farm without indoor plumbing, far away from grocery stores, and she didn't even drive. She had to be very resilient—life was hard out there on the Minnesota farm.

My mom was a godly woman who was well known for her kind and gentle character. I strive to be more like her in that respect and have some of her quality. God was faithful to her, and I'd like to keep up the family legacy of faith and trust, no matter what happens.

Her strong Christian faith was evident in her life. She was active at church, read Bible story books to us, and read her Bible daily. She was a very loving person. I had a Christian faith as a child and grew into it as I matured. I can't pinpoint a "time" when I became a Christian because it was such a normal part of daily life in our family. My mom's death didn't shake my faith like it was God's fault or something. I wasn't angry with God, just more in shock.

At the funeral, I remember one hymn in particular, called, "Have Thine Own Way, Lord," That sticks out in my mind because I was thinking, *I sure don't like this way, Lord!* My sister Nancy's high school friends provided music with singing, piano, and organ. When we went out to the cemetery, I was so impressed that Nancy's high school principal attended.

One day, when my dad had to drive us to school, we were all dashing around to get ready. My dad said, "I don't know if we can do this!" I thought, *Oh no, if Dad can't do this, I don't think we will ever make it!* He was a rock, and this must have been a rare moment of despair for him. I was close with my dad, and as a tomboy, I followed him around every chance I had, instead of helping in the house. I noticed my dad wasn't whistling while he worked in the barn anymore. It was a sad year, but by sticking together, we made it through.

My relationship with my sister Nancy was a lifeline. She didn't have the choice when it came to taking on the brunt of the responsibility. She was the oldest at home, and I felt sorry for her. Ladies from church were thoughtful and brought some meals. Our aunts helped here and there but weren't available daily. Aunt Henrietta helped where she could. One uncle, Paul, and his wife, went to garage sales and bought us clothes. Being high school girls, we didn't appreciate that very much. There weren't any grandmas close by to help out. Nancy and I depended on each other and endured our teenage years.

We didn't talk about my mom much because we were all so busy. Dad married Opal about three years after my mom died. It was my junior year of high school. I'm thankful he waited a while, and it wasn't such a fast change. We all sought to make a blended family work.

We found my mom's wedding dress, but it's crumbling. There are other things like a few wedding invitations, and some letters between my mom and our grandparents were found. We have several Christmas cards she wrote. It's nice to see her handwriting. I have some hankies given to my mom from my Grandma Siersma. Toys made by Grandpa Volkema, like a wooden wagon and stained blocks, were given to my mom for her children. Recently I copied off pictures for my daughter-in-law Katie and son Kyle, so my mom's great-grandchildren can get to know something about her.

Opal, my dad's third wife, is the grandma my kids and grandkids have known and has been very special to them.

I would have loved to share life events with my mom. You wonder what kind of grandma she'd be and what it would be like. The fact that I lost my mom so young probably has made me more of a protective mom and a little more of a worrier, or hoverer, because I realize bad things can happen.

After my mom's death, we had no choice but to go on. When you look back, it was so devastating, but the Lord got us through. My sister Nancy and I talked every day about what to wear to school and helped one another with all the household tasks. When she went to college and didn't come home every weekend, I missed her terribly. She was a natural leader and I was the follower. It would have been much harder and a different experience if we hadn't had each other.

After a close friend died years ago, I had several coffee dates with her daughter, Jodi. She wrote a diary while her mom was sick and has made her book available for people who need comfort. We did a charity walk together, called the Light of Life fund-raiser, where people could make donations to hospice. They had a memorial and lighting ceremony with luminaries, in honor of those lost that year, and later provided a seminar on Surviving the Holidays, which we attended. Grief goes in intervals, and it hit me hard to lose my friend Sandi. My mind went back to when I lost my mom when I was a teenager.

When you lose your mom early, it makes you realize how precious life is. You appreciate each moment more. I've lost several very close family members. If you've lost your mom, go easy on yourself. That longing to see your mom never really goes away no matter how long ago it was . . . it's okay. There's nothing wrong with missing her. When someone close to you dies, you think about it over and over again; it never completely disappears.

After telling my story about my mom, I realize again that it's all right under the surface, and it doesn't take much to cry. But it's so good to remember her.

We have to be thankful; God brought us through it. He didn't just go out to lunch and leave us alone when difficult things happened. He's in control.

Bible Verses:

*Indeed, he who watches over Israel will neither slumber nor sleep. The LORD watches over you—The LORD is your shade at your right hand; the sun will not harm you by day, nor the moon by night. The LORD will keep you from all harm—he will watch over your life; the LORD will watch over your coming and going both now and forevermore.* Psalm 121:4–8

We may not ever understand in this world, but God is still in control.

# IN THEIR TWENTIES WHEN MOM DIED

# Chapter 19

## Bitter or Better

## With Kari

*Kari's age at the interview was just before she turned twenty-nine years old. Her mom, Barbara, died at the age of fifty-one, on June 13, 2013, when Kari was twenty-five years old.*

My mom was hit by a car while riding her bike near 104th and Riley. The car didn't stop at the stop sign when she crossed the street. It happened very close to our house.

My husband and I were in Muskegon with friends when I got a text from my dad, wondering if I had seen my mom. I teased him that he lost his wife, because we often joke around with each other. He called me again in an hour to ask if I'd seen my mom. He and my sister had been driving around, and he called the police. It was now 9 p.m.

Then I started freaking out and thought the worst would be that she had been abducted, and we'd never find her again. I was three months pregnant, trying to stay calm, but we left and proceeded toward home. We then got a call from my dad that the police came and said she was in a car/bike accident and to meet him at Spectrum Hospital in Grand Rapids. When we were at a rest stop, my sister called my husband to tell him she was very critically injured. He didn't tell me about that call until much later.

When we arrived and stepped out of the elevator, the first thing I saw was my sister's face, and I knew our mom was no longer with us. I dropped to my knees. We went to my mom's room, but she was already gone. My dad was crying, something I had never seen before.

Only a few people knew we were pregnant with our first child. It was my parents' first grandchild. I didn't think I could do life without my mom. I was scheduled for my first doctor appointment the next day and almost didn't go, but the nurse encouraged me to come in to hear the heartbeat.

My mom was "Jane Doe" from 6:30 to 8:30 p.m. when she came to the hospital because she wasn't carrying any identification. Just before my husband and I decided to go to see our friends that evening, I considered asking my mom to go on a bike ride instead. I know when I was deciding, it was about 7 o'clock, and her accident happened at 6:30, so it wouldn't have made any difference.

None of us made it there before she died. We sat around until 2 a.m. talking together. The news stations tried my dad a few times, but he didn't answer his phone. It was all over the news that week, but thankfully we retained our privacy.

In the morning, we gathered at my dad's house. We knew we must tell my youngest sister, who was on Mackinac Island doing an internship, before she heard it elsewhere. My sister who is the middle child, and her husband, drove up there to get our youngest sister and bring her back.

Meanwhile, my dad and I made all the arrangements at the funeral home. My parents were so young they didn't have anything planned. Both of them were still working and very active.

When we did the funeral planning, my dad kept looking to me for song choices and that kind of thing. The first song that popped into my head was "In Christ Alone" because I knew she loved it and it fit with what was going on.

The first night after she died, we were all at my dad's again. The funeral director said my mom needed something to wear which covered her neck because of her injuries. While looking upstairs for some clothes for my mom to be dressed in, I walked into my old bedroom, and there was a windowpane she had recently purchased, with the words to that song, "In Christ Alone." I felt like it was a sign from God, saying, "She's okay. It's My plan, My will."

My sisters and I prepared a picture collage together, those kinds of things keep you busy and get you through. We had visitations on two nights, and so many people came, as she was highly respected and traveled to other states for her job. When you die young, most people your age are still alive to pay respects.

The funeral was awful. Our family was supposed to walk in together. It was one of the hardest moments for me because I knew they would close the casket, and it would be the last time I would see her. I was down on my knees, crying, and they tried not to rush us but kept saying, "It's time to walk down." The music kept playing over and over until we walked in. During the service, when the pastor said she was an awesome wife, mother, and grandmother, it hit me hard. The word grandmother was hard to hear. She loved kids and was so excited for her first grandson, Weston. Not having her know my son, to this day, is the worst part.

My parents took me to church my whole life, and I learned about God from an early age. My mom was active in our church and ran children's programs. In our home, they didn't show emotions openly, but they lived their Christianity more than they voiced it. I had faith as a child, but it made my faith so much stronger after my mom died. I almost hate the fact that it took going through this tragedy to make it so much more prominent in my life. A few months after she passed away, I made my profession of faith in church. The only reason I could have peace about everything was definitely God giving it to me. I believe He did everything He could to make the worst situation bearable for me.

I don't have anger about anything, even at the lady who hit her. She ran a stop sign and certainly didn't set out to kill someone that day. I think about how I'm often distracted while driving my kids and how I lean back to grab something. We know her name but have never talked to her or pressed charges. I'm feeling led to contact her in the future to let her know in person that we've forgiven her. We also know she wasn't drunk, which would have made it harder. I'm thankful God gave me a forgiving heart, so I don't have to carry the weight of anger. I don't want her to carry the weight of guilt. There are stages of grief we go through, but there's not a stage on how to cope and move on after accidentally killing a woman and being in the newspapers and news stories constantly for a couple weeks.

My only focus the first few months was taking care of my baby, my dad, and my mom's mom. One of the hardest moments was arriving at my grandma's house to tell her. She didn't take it well at all. You're not supposed to lose your children; you're supposed to die first. It was terrible to see her angry with God. It took her a long time, probably six months or more, to get through the anger. By God's grace, she came to a place of peace.

God gave me such a feeling of peace, even though I missed my mom. Seeing her in heaven is something I have to look forward to. Even when I was crying all the time, I had a sense of calm deep inside. It helped that God gave us a baby to anticipate in six months. Weston was a bit of a surprise to us, and I can't wait to share with him someday what his life really did for all of us! Due to my mom's death I worried about my husband if he was late getting home from work, to the point I would call friends and family looking for him.

Often, I think of an illustration our pastor once did. He showed a long rope from one end of the sanctuary to the other end. The first end was colored red for a few inches and symbolized the day you were conceived and your entire life on earth. He said to imagine that the white part of the rope would go on forever, symbolizing eternal life. It really put things into perspective for me. The marked part of the rope was such a little part. I have so much more time to spend with my mom in eternity, which goes on forever, and the part here on earth is so short.

Since I know life can change in a second, I make sure I say, "I love you," to my kids often. I think in a strange way, this all made me more alive. I'm doing my best to live every moment to the fullest.

I'm very glad my mom knew about my pregnancy before she died. We weren't going to tell them yet, but it came out and my mom was so excited. I wish she could have been around for the birth of my sons. I miss her at Christmastime because she loved it and made such a big deal of it. Now that we have kids, it makes it easier because they keep you busy and make you laugh.

My mom and I were incredibly close. It was normal for us to call, email, or text multiple times daily. I've kept them all, and they're special to me. I love reading through them. One of my favorite memories happened the day before she died. She sent pink and blue balloons anonymously to my work but never did confess to it. That's the way my coworkers found out I was pregnant. Later, although difficult, we did find out she sent them.

I'm very intentional about being involved with my kids. I've already set up an email account for each of them, and I write letters and send pictures to them, even though my boys are very young. If I die early, they will have that. My mom was a busy working mom and didn't make picture books or baby books, but my parents attended every event we had.

My mom and I had such a great relationship and could talk about anything. I miss her advice, although she had an annoying way of getting me to talk about a situation until I figured it out on my own. But that prepared me for life, made me more independent, and was a blessing. She taught me by her example, how to be strong and loving at the same time. I don't think strong women often know how to show us the soft loving part, but she did.

We did so many things together, such as shopping, tennis, games, and camping. We took several excursions and trips over the years, like Disney World, cruises, and Petoskey, Michigan. When I lived at home for a few years after college, I was dating my future husband. He and my mom were so close, he would tease her, go to her for advice, and would often talk with her a while after walking in the door, before he came to find me. I loved seeing the two of them interact and joke around with each other as if they were family even before he and I were married.

We took all of my mom's shirts to a place called Living Threads. They make quilts out of clothes after someone passes away. We had twelve quilts made, just in case, for her grandchildren and one for my dad. They're so professionally made, and the donations go to charity. They explained how my mom is living on by helping people who suffer poverty in other countries.

Several instances come up where I feel I can help others going through this. A gal I know on Facebook messaged me when her dad passed away.

A work friend's dad had a sudden heart attack and died. I talk to people or just listen. They know I get it. God puts people in front of me, and I try to assist them.

If you've lost your mother, it's never easy. Even after a few years, sometimes that drive to work alone after dropping off my kids, if the right song is playing, I break down and cry. I can turn these moments off sooner than I used to be able to. I know this was God's plan from day one. It doesn't make sense, but it doesn't have to. That's actually the beauty in it sometimes. He will use this situation if you open up to the possibility of the number of people you may be able to help in the world. Because of the traumatic situation you've just overcome, your heart will be full and spill over in love for others.

I'm much more comfortable talking about death now, and some might think that's morbid. I'm sure some would think it almost sounds suicidal, but I would be fine with going to heaven now, but the only thing that makes me want to stay longer is I don't want my kids to go through this pain. You don't get it until you go through it.

Talking about my mom has been so good for me. I never went to therapy. I spent the entire first year making sure everyone else was okay. I had one child, then the next, so I didn't think much. I haven't taken the time to focus or see how far I've come since that horrible day.

Here's a quote by my former pastor, Dann Stouten:

"Faith is lived out in the everydayness of life, but it's tested in the fire of a handful of defining moments. In those few moments, we must decide if what has happened to us will make us bitter or better. Will hardship drive a wedge between us and God, or will it drive us into His waiting arms? Choosing to believe in such moments causes the saints to rejoice and the angels to dance." It paints a beautiful picture of heaven and the choice that I have made.

Bible verse:

*You saw me before I was born. The days allotted to me had all been recorded in your book, before any of them ever began.* Psalm 139:16 GNB

# Chapter 20

## A Challenging Childhood

## With Elaine Stock

*Elaine's mother, Sandra, died at the age of forty-six, in the late 1980's.*

My mother left our family in the middle of the night, without forewarning, when I was sixteen, my brother was fourteen. A few years later my parents agreed upon a divorce, and she lived in San Francisco for years. Except for occasional phone calls and letters, there was little communication between us. She was in California when she passed away. I was married and resided in New York.

My mother was diagnosed with stage four ovarian cancer one year before she died. She wrote a letter saying the doctor had found "changing cells." She planned to drink plenty of orange juice to get better. Sadly, it didn't work.

We were not separated just by distance, but were also emotionally separated. This emotional estrangement began years ago when I was a child. There were times when she was near hysteria in fear of gangs of people chasing after us . . . packs of dogs as well. She often sequestered herself away from us, from almost anyone, and remained in her bedroom for hours. The tension between my parents grew and festered. It wasn't until she relocated to San Francisco that she was diagnosed with paranoid schizophrenia.

My mother wasn't a violent person, but troubled. Medications to treat her sufficiently were not available then. She tried her best to be a good mother to my brother and me, but her mental illness controlled and limited her. One fond memory I have of her as a loving mother is centered on her joy of reading. Weekly, she took us to the library. She made a delightful big production when I was old enough to receive my first library card. Sadly though, days like our excursions to the library would begin as fun, but they usually ended badly.

Looking back, I can say she was a direct influence on my love of reading, and perhaps, why I'm now a published author. She also loved the arts and culture and often took us to museums and parks. She had a creative side, dabbled in poetry and enjoyed music. These are a glimpse of a few good memories I have, but invariably they were laced with emotional detachment or scary moments due to her paranoia and delusions. As a child, I believed there really were animals that were about to attack us and didn't know they were only conjured within my mother's mind.

I had to do many things by myself as a young child. One experience, in particular, is still haunting—if I allow it to eclipse me in sadness. That's the time when I had to ride a city bus to my dance recital, dressed in costume, because my parents weren't there for me. My father worked; my mother couldn't leave the house. Honestly, I'm not playing the sad fiddle. Being the daughter of a schizophrenic was not easy. Although I've overcome some of the fears my mother instilled in me, I still face some daily.

My self-esteem was also greatly impacted by my mother's illness. After high school graduation, I visited my mother in San Francisco. She played tourist with me, and we had a nice time going all over the city. Yet, it was a difficult time, our reactions ping-ponged between us. Here I was, about to go to college, intending to go into family counseling. She was negative and discouraging, and questioned my motives and ability to achieve this based upon the fact, which she admitted, that my lack of a good personal childhood and happy family experiences would not help others. Also, I'd grown my hair long. She said she didn't like it. It might sound like a personal opinion that she certainly was entitled to have, but all throughout my childhood she spoke negatively about how I looked. That's the way it usually went with her. This additional assessment of hers was one more hurt, that for better or worse, I internalized.

I was brought up in a faithless family. If my parents believed in God, they didn't show it or teach it. They were not atheists or hateful toward Him, but they didn't acknowledge a loving God. Yet, very early in my life, I knew there was a God. I can't remember a situation or a person who influenced me, but I was very blessed that He made His presence known to me.

In my late teens, I was searching for wholeness in my empty-feeling life. When I met and married my husband, I gave my life to the Lord and was baptized into the Christian faith. We attend church and enjoy growing in our faith.

When I was in my late twenties, I learned from my mother's boyfriend of her health deterioration. She was in the hospital, dying. The last time I spoke to her was when I phoned her about a week before her passing. When a nurse answered, my first reaction was, "Oh no, she's gone already!" Instead, the nurse said, "I'll put her on," and gave her the receiver. Whether from the morphine, or her schizophrenia, or both, she was hysterical and screamed into the phone. She was totally incoherent and not making sense. To this day, I wish I had never heard those last words.

Perhaps I was in denial, but I debated visiting with her during her final days. My husband and I had gone out to see her just a month prior. She was still coherent then and was able to talk, but it was very awkward. There were no tender or loving words. Even when she was younger, she never expressed herself that way.

The expected call from her boyfriend finally came one day when I arrived home from work: My mother had passed away. She was buried in California; there was no funeral. Her boyfriend oversaw everything, and he did not plan one. Since there was a problem with her identification, she couldn't be moved out of the hospital morgue for many days. I kept having a disturbing picture in my mind of her in a refrigerated compartment with a toe tag on.

I was in a state of shock for a while. My mind went numb. After two weeks, the emotions started to sink in, and I cried my eyes out in a delayed reaction. To be honest, to this day, I wish for the emotionally giving and externally loving mother I never had.

The minister at our church agreed when I asked him if we could have some sort of memorial service for my mother. It was important for me to have a Christian memorial service. It was something I could do to make me feel connected to God about her death, even though she wasn't connected to God. To this day, I still don't think I have total closure about the past or my mother, but I did experience a sense of relief from this memorial service. Sometimes when it gets to me, I have to get busy and not think about the past that cannot be changed.

My faith was the only thing that got me through the sad loss of my mother. I was a new Christian then, of about five years. As a child, I had faith in God that I clung to. As a young adult, I latched onto Jesus' hand and never let go. I also had a job that made me get up, go to work, and do everyday things. I couldn't stay home and be depressed, couldn't—wouldn't—feel sorry for myself. The only day I give myself a pass is on Mother's Day. Right or wrong, I'm unable emotionally to attend church on that Sunday. It doesn't help that my mother died on Friday the 13th of Mother's Day Weekend. All the attention is focused on moms and how wonderful and necessary they are in a child's life. Perhaps it's also difficult because I don't have children of my own. Yet, as time moves forward and I get older, I realize everyone has some type of complication in their lives. We all have a different story to tell.

This past Mother's Day (at the time of this interview) was the first time I posted a tribute on social media about my mother. I shared a photo of my parents holding me and looking at each other lovingly. I also put a poem on my blog for my mother. I don't hate my mother. She was a very ill person. Once she told me: "If there were any way to get rid of this illness I would." That was before she was officially diagnosed with schizophrenia.

I would have appreciated having a relationship with my mother and hearing her say, "How about having lunch today?" Or saying to her, "My job is upsetting me, can we talk?" Having someone to be a confidant, someone to talk to as an adult would have been great. Or on a fun basis, like, "Hey, how about going shopping or seeing a movie tomorrow?"

Something I wish I could ask my mother is, "Do you love me?" I know she did deep down, but I wish I would have heard those words from her. Internally, I know God loves me as His beloved daughter and wants me to trust Him with all my life issues. I feel God asking, "Do you trust Me, or don't you trust Me, yes or no?" I do trust Him fully. And that means He wanted me to have the parents He gave me. No mistakes made!

Some people have told me, "I've lost my mother too." In some situations, I've shared part of my personal story but am careful not to hurt others and to honor my family. I've spoken about my mother and have tried to encourage others. I try not to be the center of the world—implying, poor me, look at me, my life stinks. I also emphasize that my mother didn't act the way she did because she was an evil, abusive parent. She was a very ill woman. Friends know they can talk to me, and I will be a listening ear.

My mother's death changed me by giving me somewhat of a wake-up call. I was in my late twenties and enjoyed writing. It seemed as if God was saying, "Do you want to do anything about it?" My mother didn't do much with the arts she adored. I felt like God told me, "If you want to do it, get going. Time is not going to stop." Now I write with more urgency.

These days, I make myself move forward to face my tomorrows. Actually, that's a theme that's seen in my stories—with hope and faith, one can face better tomorrows no matter the circumstances.

I encourage women to talk about losing their mothers and their troubling relationships. Don't keep it bottled up. Accept that it hurts, and you don't really ever get over it, but you need to continue on. If you have extended family and resources you can count on, then lean on them to get through the difficult times. If you're a mother, love your children intensely and build a strong relationship with them. Most of all, look to God. I've had to trust in God and rely on Him. He's always there for me.

I'm telling my story in the hope that it can be an encouragement to women in similar situations. God's arms are always open to embrace you as His daughter.

Bible verse:

*Be strong and courageous. Do not be afraid; do not be discouraged, for the LORD your God will be with you wherever you go.* Joshua 1:9

# Chapter 21

## Spending Quality Time With Karen Blakley

*Karen's age at the time of the interview was fifty-eight. Karen was twenty years old, when her mom, Mary, passed away at the age of sixty, in 1977.*

I was living in Allegan, Michigan, working as a nurse at Allegan Hospital on the evening shift. About 2 a.m. I got a call that my mom had passed away, which was such a shock because I didn't even know she was in the hospital.

My dad was on the phone first but couldn't talk; then my oldest sister, Patty, said it. "Mom died." I said, "What??" I threw on clothes and went straight to my parents' house.

My mom was born in 1916 and was a child of the depression, so when she was young, she had to quit work and take care of her siblings. When I was young, I wasn't interested in hearing about things like my mom's childhood, but now I'm curious about what it was like.

I can count on one hand the number of times I missed church in my childhood. You had to be down in bed or in the hospital to miss a Sunday. My mom had a strong Christian faith, although not expressive about it. She always said, "God is in control of everything."

My mom's life was busy and tiring but full of enthusiasm. She was an excellent cook, but back then it was expected to have dinner on the table after a long day at work. Every Sunday noon she made a big dinner, and sometimes other relatives and friends came too. She was very sociable and enjoyed a lot of people around her. She was a people gatherer. Our house was always full and even if it was messy, she didn't care.

She was so proud that my sisters and I went to college. Mom wrote me faithfully while I was in Grand Rapids for nursing school. I kept a couple of those letters. There was only one phone on the wall in our dorm floor. Long-distance phone calls were expensive.

Along with the letters, I have some photos, a whole glassware set, and a cedar chest. My mom's little childhood prayer book, a photo of her in her pretty dress when she was young, a necklace with her name on it, and several other trinkets in a shadow box are meaningful to me. An embroidered pillowcase and some afghans and baby blankets she made are in the cedar chest.

My mom taught me to be generous with my time and with the gifts God has given me. She didn't have many material possessions, but she had time for people. Quality time. That's something I remember most, not cooking skills or something, but appreciating people.

My mom's death came very suddenly. She had some minor heart issues over the years, but she was living a normal, active life. She worked all day at the Dog Life plant in Hamilton, and began to have chest pain in the evening. My youngest sister drove her to Holland Hospital.

They thought it was angina and not a heart attack but admitted her overnight. My mom said, "Oh, you don't need to call Karen. She's working. We'll call her tomorrow."

My dad and sister went home to sleep, as she was scheduled to have tests the next day. Medical science wasn't as advanced then, so when she had some heart problems previously, nothing was done for her. Now they might have done stents or surgeries. She was a very busy wife, mom of six children, and grandmother of five.

At my parents' home the night she died, we all sat in shock. We were a "huggy" family and wanted to be together. We went with my dad the next day to do the planning at the funeral home. It's not something you want to do. It all happened so suddenly. I think she died on a Thursday and the funeral was on Saturday.

Since my mom was well-liked and could make friends with anyone of any age, the visitations were very busy. We stood near the open coffin while people came to talk to us. She was a knitter and made baby sweaters and afghans for others. She was an extrovert, loved to be out and about, and was the life of the party. She knitted every chance she had; I can still hear the "click, click" of the needles. Many people mentioned that. A man she knew at work even told us that she had given him money when he was in great need. Not a lot, but she did it anyway, although she didn't have any extra to give. Those kinds of comments are so helpful at funeral visitations.

I was already married and expecting my first child when my mom died. She died in February, a month after I told her about the pregnancy. My oldest sister had knowledge of infant care, which was a great help to me. When my daughter was born in August, she came over to help. All of my sisters were a comfort to me. We grew closer after our mother's death, but most of them didn't live close. Mom was making a baby blanket when she died. I like to think it was for me. Mom's friend finished it, and I used it for all of my babies.

It was very difficult for me to see my grandma, my mom's mom, go through losing her daughter. She was around eighty, and of course it seems so unnatural for your children to die first. When we visited Grandma, she just cried. I think it was harder on her than anyone else, and it seemed she never got over it. Of course, it was hard on us to lose a mom, but you have to go on because you're busy with your own growing family, and you expect your parents to die before you do.

As a young person, I seemed to have head knowledge of Jesus, but not heart knowledge. I certainly knew God. Without Jesus fully in my heart at the time of the funeral, I was so devastated because I would never see my mom again. It was a wailing grief. For about seven years after my mom's death, I struggled with God and had lots of discussions with Him. My mom's death seemed so unfair. I also had to go through a divorce. That difficult season in my life finally brought me to the realization that I couldn't make it without clinging to the Lord. Hard times can build your faith. I'm sure I wouldn't have the same reaction now. I certainly would grieve, but it wouldn't be a hopeless grief.

Now I really do appreciate people more. Knowing how quickly things can change, I'm sure I'm more serious than I would have been. I didn't smother my children—they're all independent and doing well, but the reality is that anything can happen to them or me at any moment. I don't take anyone for granted anymore.

Something I did in honor of my mom was that I selected a World Vision child to sponsor, who was born on the exact day my mom died. His name is Patrick. When I correspond with him, it reminds me of her. I wanted to make her death date a pleasant day. God redeemed the day.

I try to be a listening ear and empathetic to those who have lost a parent. Lots of my friends are now beginning to lose them. Your mom is always your mom. She will be your cheerleader no matter what you do, if you've had a good relationship. I have a friend who lost her mom suddenly around Mother's Day a few years ago. I went to the funeral visitation, and there's nothing we can do to make it better, but we can be a comforting presence for them.

My oldest sister found reel-to-reel tapes of our family and had them made into DVDs. There were some of my mom when she was young, on my grandfather's farm, various other relatives and friends, the blueberry farm they had, cows, and the garden. One of the videos had one of my mom's friends, Jean, on it. She has died now, and I ran into her daughter and later gave her a copy of it. She was thrilled and cried. She didn't have any visual of her mom other than a few pictures. It was such a blessing to her, and you would have thought I gave her the world.

God comforted me one particular year in an unexpected way. At one point, I realized my mom had been gone more years of my life than she was here. It was the anniversary of her death. I was very teary because it didn't seem like I could remember what she sounded like or what she smelled like anymore. I went to our evening service at church, which I didn't do regularly. A lady slid in the pew next to me. It was a best friend of my mom's. She hadn't even seen me, she just happened to sit there. I said, "Alice?" She knew what the date was, and we hugged. It was such a God-thing. She told me some things about my mom and comforted me. She said, "Your mom surely loved Jesus!" Since then, Alice has died. It was such a blessing to meet with her. She and Mom must have had heart to heart talks. My mom lived a difficult life and probably needed talks with Alice. It was a beautiful moment to meet her. She gave me so much hope twenty years after my mom died.

My daughter works with hospice, and she's been nearby many times when people pass away. She observes, sometimes it's horrible, other times it's a sadness but not hopeless. There's such a huge difference between believers and nonbelievers and their families, when a person dies.

It's a hard thing to live most of your life without your mother. But there is hope. I know I will see her again in heaven and we'll all be reunited one day. God's end of the story is a wonderful one. I have blessed assurance because of Jesus Christ.

Bible Verse:

*When you pass through the waters, I will be with you; and when you pass through the rivers, they will not sweep over you. When you walk through the fire, you will not be burned; the flames will not set you ablaze. For I am the LORD your God, the Holy One of Israel, your Savior. Isaiah 43:2–3*

This verse has been helpful to me in many situations including when I've grieved my mom's death.

# Chapter 22

## Light Shines Brightest in the Dark

### With Rachael Smith

*Rachael was thirty-eight years old at the time of the interview. Rachael was twenty-four when her mom Elaine, died at the age of fifty-four, in July of 2003.*

My mom had been feeling sick for a while—very tired and uncomfortable. She was seeing her doctor, and nothing was found. She began having these bizarre facial swellings, and she looked terrible, to the point she wouldn't let anyone see her. They tried taking her off a blood pressure medicine she was on. She still had facial swelling and flu-like symptoms. Back at her doctor, she cried and demanded they figure out why she was so sick. The doctor said she was just depressed. We were angry because that was a result, not a cause. She was adamant. The doctor finally did blood work after my mom had asked for solutions for months. That was March of 2003, and she had already been feeling bad at the previous Christmas.

Even before she got the blood work back, she got much sicker. My husband and I were in the process of moving from Louisville, Kentucky, where I grew up, to Atlanta. I called my mom, and she didn't sound right and hadn't for a long time. That was the last time I had a normal conversation with her.

The next day was Sunday. My husband and I went to church and then to his parents for dinner. This was just before we had cell phones. My family had a very difficult time contacting us but finally found us. They called in a panic, requesting us to come to the hospital immediately. We rushed to see my mom in the critical care unit.

What I didn't know until later was that after I got off the phone with her the night before, my mom vomited blood and collapsed. At the hospital, they determined she was bleeding into her stomach. They thought it was a bleeding ulcer and treated her for that. My dad went home to sleep because she seemed to be stable. He planned to bring her clothes in the morning.

Early the next morning they called my dad and said he needed to get to the hospital right away. Many complications caused my mom to be taken into emergency surgery. They had to take out some organs and found a mass the size of a football. They took out what they could, closed her back up, and put her in a drug-induced coma so her body would rest. They didn't expect her to come out of the coma, but after three weeks, she did. She was diagnosed with non-Hodgkin's lymphoma, which is a very treatable cancer. But because the doctor hadn't found it earlier, it was allowed to grow and cause a great amount of damage in her body.

They tried a new experimental drug while she was still in the coma. Chemotherapy kills cancer cells but also good cells. We thought, *Oh my goodness! She may still survive this!* But cancer spread throughout her body. She was getting weaker and then had ICU psychosis, which is when your mind is filled with hallucinations because of the trauma. She came out of that eventually and was coherent for a time.

When my mom was in critical care, one of my friends complained about her own health problems when she visited. Another friend would call and say she was bringing Subway. It was so appreciated because she didn't ask me to make a big decision, she just said she was bringing food, then sat with me and didn't expect anything. This reminded me how to help someone in a practical way.

I didn't want to go ahead with our move to Atlanta, but with my dad's persuading, my husband and I moved. He said my mom wouldn't want us to put our lives on hold for her. She survived two rounds of chemo and was doing occupational therapy. They were preparing her to go home. On the surface, it seemed she was holding her own, but she was very sick. I have few regrets in life, but that is one. I wish we had waited to move.

At the end of June, she told my dad, "I'm going home in four weeks." After a couple weeks, my dad realized she was right, her scheduled release was exactly four weeks from the time she said that. After the next round of chemo, she didn't recover. Within days, she was gone. She died four weeks to the day from when she said that to my dad.

We were in Atlanta, and my family kept calling me to come home because my mom was failing. We didn't know what to do. Now that we had moved, we were ingrained. I had a new job as a dental hygienist, and my husband was in school. My office manager was a widowed woman about the age of my parents. She said, "Rachael, go home. You will either go home and be part of the celebration that she's improving, or that you need to be home." In the middle of the night, I got a call from my sister that she was gone. I regretted I wasn't home. We had moved less than a month before that. I'm the only one of my siblings that didn't get to say goodbye to her.

We gathered at my dad's house. We felt betrayal and anger towards the doctor who didn't catch it in the first place. I also had anger toward God. It was the first time I lost someone close, I had moved, and nothing in my life was stable at that point. Our family discussed how we had faith that she would be healed. I think there was a general feeling of disappointment in how everything went. I felt a disconnect with God for the first time, thinking about, *What does the passage even mean, about having faith to be healed? Is it about God doing something for me, or is it that God is who He says He is, regardless of what happens?* It was a trust issue.

I really clung to the song, "Blessed Be the Name of the Lord," which had only been out a short while. We often sang it at my church, and while everyone else was standing and singing, I huddled in my seat in tears. To say that you believe, and then to actually live it, is a different thing.

We had a couple nights of funeral visitation. There were nonstop people. A few things were stressful. I had a former coworker who had recently lost her mother, who was understanding. But some came through that weren't acting like they were at a funeral visitation at all, and were cutting up. I didn't feel like pretending or entertaining them.

At the funeral, I was numb. It was meaningful that my husband sang, "I Can Only Imagine," by MercyMe. Since the funeral, I can't listen to that song without crying. It wasn't planned, but my dad spoke about the fact that she said she was going home in four weeks. She did go home, to heaven. It was all heartbreaking but special at the same time.

After her death I often talked to God, saying, "You allowed this awful thing to happen, so what's the point of it? God, how are you going to redeem this?" He doesn't have to reveal it to me. He's certainly not required to, but years later He did. He knew where my faith was at the time, and the gracious Lord that He is, he met me where my faith was in order to strengthen it. I had to have faith that He is who He says He is. That's where I had to trust. It took me a long time to get there. If He hadn't shown me, I don't think I could have reconciled that He's a good, loving God. I wasn't there yet. It was the first major terrible thing that happened in my life. I had a pretty cushy life. Finally, life got real. I grew up with the health and wealth type of preaching. Then in college, I got away from it. I searched the scriptures, saying, "I am reading this and what did you really say about this God?" I felt that God didn't hold up His end of the bargain.

While preparing to do a fundraiser race for lymphoma, I met a gal in Atlanta who began running with me, because we had the same pace. She wasn't a Christian when we met, but later, she began going to church with us and grew in faith. At some point, I realized that if my mom hadn't died when she did and the way she did, I would have never met Karen. She was my redemption. I'm not glad my mom died, but scripture says He will redeem our lives. He will take the hurt and ugliness and mend it.

When I was young, I witnessed that my mom was always in the Word and praying. She would say, "I'm going in my room to pray, you may not come get me for one hour." Now that I'm a mom of three young children, I understand the importance of praying for them. She was a fighter when she prayed. I always knew my mom was warring for me. My mom taught me how to love fiercely with prayers of healing and protection. When I heard her pray out loud it was a passionate spiritual battle. I felt the Holy Spirit's presence strongly.

As a young person I was so self-absorbed, I didn't care about hearing anything from my mom. During college, the fog started to lift. When I got married, I realized she was actually a person, with wisdom to share. I haven't arrived, but continually see things more clearly now and would love to sit down with her to hear her advice or experiences. We did so many things together, such as watching funny movies, sewing, and almost anything DIY. We worked in the garden and did canning. I got to keep her canning materials, her Precious Moments figurines, her wedding rings, and a scrapbook I made about her. She was hardly ever spontaneous, but, one time, just before Christmas, when I was around ten, we were coming home in the car, just the two of us. She said, "You know what? Let's just drive around and look at the Christmas lights!" It's one of my fondest memories.

For a while after my mom's death, I was in a pretty dark place. I went to a counselor who was a great help. She advised me not to be so busy, as that's one of my tendencies. In the book she recommended, *A Grace Disguised*, by Sitzer, he described the loss of his wife, mother, and daughter in one accident. He talked about running straight into the darkness, instead of chasing the light. I needed to run into the darkness so I could get to the light because the light shines brightest in the dark. I needed to enter into the pain and let God shine His light on my sorrow.

My dad got remarried some years later, but I talk about my mom to my kids. They know she was important to me, and they ask questions about her now. It helps that my dad's wife isn't afraid to talk about her. She is respectful of my mom and puts flowers on her gravestone. She always wanted to be a grandma and is appreciative of being woven into our family.

The loss of my mother sparked fears about mothering my own children. I thought, *I don't want to do it without my mom!* When we lived in Atlanta, I craved a mentor in my life, so I started praying about it. One day, as I was chatting with a patient, she said she had been praying about whether she should mentor young women. I told her I had been praying for a mentor. We began to meet for coffee or lunch once a week. We were in touch for a few years but now no longer are in contact. She was a huge influence in my life when I badly needed a mother figure.

The first few years after my mom's death, my family and I did something big on the anniversary of her death, such as hang gliding one year. Maybe it was a distraction, or to redeem the day by doing something positive. As the years went on, we didn't do that much, but I always remember her on the day.

I recently met a new friend who lost her mom a short time ago, so it's fresh. We're in the same small group. I've reached out to her. I want to let her know she's not alone and someone gets it. On that first Mother's Day you don't have your mom, it's awful. When people ask, "How long does it last?" I know it sounds pessimistic, but I tell them you don't stop missing them. It's freeing and brings acceptance that it's okay to feel that way.

I love praising and singing. I feel like that's what heaven is—worshipping. When I'm worshipping, I feel so close to my mom because I know in that moment, we are doing the same thing and we're doing it together. If I'm in a mood when I'm really missing her, I just praise, and then I know I'm with her.

If your mother has passed away, it's okay to mourn. Don't be afraid to run into the darkness. Being that I'm a writer, I've shared a lot of this before in written and spoken form. I actually love to tell the story. It's therapeutic for me to talk about her.

Bible Verses:

*You, Lord, took up my case; you redeemed my life.* Lamentations 3:58

*Rejoice with those who rejoice, weep with those who weep.* Romans 12:15 ESV

I think so many people try to fix it because they're uncomfortable with grief. I say, "I'm not going to try to cheer you up; I'll sit and cry with you."

# Chapter 23

# Caught Up Together in the Clouds

## With Vanessa Jorge

*Vanessa was twenty-nine at the time of the interview. She was twenty-six, when her mom, Laura, died at the age of sixty-eight years old, on December 23, 2013.*

Because I was still living at my parents' home in New Jersey, I was very involved with my mom's illness. My half-siblings are a lot older, and I was the only one somewhat available daily. At the time she was diagnosed, I attended college, a half-hour drive from our home. During the week I was out at school or work for the day, but at night and on weekends I was helping my folks.

My mom went through a series of diagnoses and treatments over four years. It started with a bad cough. She was seeing many doctors and was diagnosed with a rare pulmonary condition. We went to doctors in Philadelphia, New Jersey, and New York. Then she was diagnosed with myelodysplastic syndrome (MDS), a blood disorder. Unfortunately, my mother wasn't a candidate for treatment because of her preexisting conditions. Her MDS developed into acute leukemia. They gave her aggressive chemotherapy, which probably bought her some time, but she suffered being very tired and sick. In and out of many hospitals, the last year became a blur. The specialists suggested we put her on hospice care.

We let her decide, and she chose to keep fighting. My father and I took her to New York Presbyterian Cancer Center, where they do research. She spent two months there.

At first, it looked like she was improving while in New York. She went into a procedure to check her lungs. While under anesthesia she suffered a stroke. When she woke up, she couldn't open her eyes, had trouble breathing, and her left side was paralyzed. This is when I came to the realization that this battle was over. We fought so long for her to get better, and I think this was a sign from God saying it was time to let her go. I felt guilty saying that and kept telling her how sorry I was for bringing her there. She was cooped up in the hospital in pain, and if I had put her on hospice care, she would have passed away by that time.

Near the end of my mom's life, my commute from work, to the hospital, to home was done on autopilot due to the chaos. My seventy-two-year-old dad, who was a cancer survivor, went in for a routine colonoscopy and had complications. He became a patient in a different hospital but got released to see my mom on her last days.

After a talk with her doctor, we made the decision to give my mom morphine to make her comfortable and let her go on her own. We didn't know if it would take a day or a week. My brother was there with her and convinced me to go home to get a shower and a bag. When I arrived at home, he called me to hurry back as her blood pressure was going down.

When I returned to my mom's side, I had a few hours with her, holding her hand, and telling her I was sorry, but we did the best we could. I was so thankful I got back in time, and couldn't have lived with myself if I wasn't there with her. I told her I would be okay and gave her permission to go. She told me often before her stroke, that the only reason she fought so hard was for me. She passed away at 7:05 p.m. that evening.

After a week, we had a simple memorial back in New Jersey. She wanted cremation with her ashes at the church. We also had a little get-together at the house for whoever could come. After the funeral, it all hit me like a bomb. A few months later, my father and I had a private burial of her ashes at a local mausoleum. It's nice to have a place to go to honor her.

Over time, I have let go of most regrets. Those last four days after the stroke was the worst part for me. It was the most hopeless I've ever felt. The whole time it seemed I had some sort of control over her sickness, and we could make her more comfortable. But once we got to that point, I felt it was very much out of my hands.

After a time, I knew I was in a deep depression and needed to go to counseling. I didn't have much support around me. My best friend was helpful, but I realized after a while she didn't know what to tell me, and I felt like I was rambling on. I saw a therapist for a year and then spread the appointments out. There were days I couldn't sleep, when I couldn't get out of bed, or I had extreme anxiety when I went to a grocery store or out in public. I was placed on a medication for a while. I always wondered why other people couldn't just cope with things instead of going on medication. I've never been a fan of them but realized I needed something to hold me over until I could transition back into normal life. Being in that position myself taught me that I needed some help to get emotionally stable. Exercise was something I'd always done to de-stress, but when my mom was sick, I got out of the habit because I simply did not have time. Exercising and eating healthier again helped me. I also did extensive journaling to get my feelings out. I went to group therapy too, which was very helpful. The others could understand because they were going through similar things.

Therapy helped me to conquer my guilt about my mom. When you're a teenager, you're all about yourself. Even though I wasn't severely rebellious, for a time, I wasn't close to my mom. When you mature you realize what's important in life, and in my late teens I started to appreciate my mom more. In my early twenties we became very close friends. You think you have so many more years to enjoy the relationship. It was like two women having fun and enjoying life together. It turned out that it was short-lived. Part of my regret was I wish I'd recognized the importance of my mother earlier, so I had more time to enjoy her.

My mom taught me about God from an early age, and we went to church every Sunday. When she got sick, she really hung onto her faith, and I did too. It comes to a breaking point when you accept whatever God has planned for you. I think she accepted it and let go before she had her stroke.

After she died, I tried to keep my mother's voice in my head, to remember how she told me to stand on my own two feet and be independent. She wouldn't want me to stay in the gutter and depressed for long. She would want me to rise above and live a happy, strong life. Most of all, my mom wanted me to be self-sufficient, not solely dependent on a man financially or emotionally. She hoped I would have a husband one day that respects me, but that I would take care of myself and hold my head up high. She also felt that it was very important to be a good person and treat others well.

To me, my mother was perfect, but I realize she had flaws like everyone else. I think that's why I was in denial when she first got sick, because I felt she was practically immortal and could get through anything and was hoping it was just a bump in the road for her. When she continued to get sicker, it really rocked my world. I tell people, the day my mother passed away, a big part of me passed away with her. I'm not anywhere near the same person I was.

Now I have my own place, have a healthy relationship with my boyfriend, and a good job. In some ways, I've changed to the better, the way my mom would have wanted. I'm not going to lie: initially, after my mom passed away, I went through some horrible times. Before the therapy I had trouble processing it all, and my faith was very shaken. I thought my mother was such a good person and didn't deserve to be taken out so soon and it wasn't fair. She deserved to live her older years, watch me get married, and enjoy grandchildren. I want to be a mother at some point, and when the time comes, I'm going to be petrified since my mom's not here for it.

My mom told story after story about her mom. I never knew my grandmother, but I still feel a spiritual connection with her, because my mom told me so much about her. My mom told me about her relationship with her mom when she was growing up, how my grandmother was a nurse, and even the love story between my grandparents. I felt bad that my future children won't have their grandmother around either, but I will tell them all about her.

I'm young, and I think about all the milestones I have ahead of me. When I got my first apartment, I wondered what she would think of it. When I get married or start a family, I wish she could be here for those. I met my boyfriend on my birthday four months after she passed away. I thought he would just be a friend, and I was still not in a good mental state. But he was a huge support for me to get through that time. He actually reminds me of my mother because he has a very nurturing and caring nature.

If I could, I would ask her to forgive me of my mistakes. I hope she wasn't in pain on her last few days. On the death date, I usually take off work and go to the cemetery to sit a while, then in the evening take time to reflect and go through pictures and mementos of her. She loved wine, so I tip a glass in honor of her.

After my mom passed away, I struggled with the bad memories of her suffering. I couldn't get them out of my mind. I had to learn how to replace those memories with good memories. I tried to play a good memory in my mind of the time we went away together only two months before she died, on a gorgeous October day. She happened to have a weekend when she felt pretty good, but her gray hair was coming in. We both decided to get our hair done, ate at an outdoor restaurant, and went shopping.

Her urn came in a pretty memory box with black suede cloth on the inside, which I kept to store special things. I kept her cell phone, a dried flower from the floral arrangement, hair I took from her hairbrush in a little box, her hospital bracelet, some pictures of when she was young, and a card she wrote to me when I was in college. I love seeing her handwriting. She wrote about how proud she was of me. I also kept the last card I wrote to her for her birthday. An exercise we had to do in group therapy was to write a letter from the perspective of the person who passed away. I wrote a letter about what she might say to me. She would say she was proud of me, to be strong no matter what happened, and that she was doing fine in heaven.

Initially, when my mom passed, I didn't think it would ever be possible to be happy again. I have great hope now, as I've gotten through the worst part of my grieving. I keep good people around me, do things I've dreamed of doing, and keep moving forward, doing all I can to make my mother proud. I've decided to live my life more fully.

Now I do some volunteering to raise money for the lymphoma society for cancer research. As part of my therapy, I raised one thousand dollars and ran my first 10K run. I get donations in my mom's name, it keeps me in shape, and I'm doing something useful.

Even though I don't need the group therapy sessions anymore, I still go occasionally. There are some girls around my age whose mothers have passed away, and I can really relate to how they're feeling. I share my story, and hopefully, I help them in some way. I'm just a few steps ahead of them in the journey.

The death of my mom forced me to grow up much faster than I would have. Death isn't something on your mind in your twenties. My mother was so vibrant, outgoing, and hardworking, and to see her pass away so suddenly, you realize how precious every day is. I have to be careful to prioritize and continue to take care of myself. I want to be around for the next generation. If I have children, I want to see them graduate, get married, and have their own kids, which won't be possible if my health declines.

It's okay to feel horrible when your mom passes away. You have to give yourself permission to feel whatever it is you need to feel. You might be angry at the world or yourself for a time. Everybody grieves at their own pace. If it takes you a couple years, or yours passes more quickly than others, don't feel like you're abnormal.

Before, I was trying to be in control as much as I could. Now her passing has taught me to let go and let God take the wheel. If I hadn't learned this, I'd still be in the same black hole as I was a few years ago. I pray a lot more than I used to. Now I put a lot more of my life into God's hands. You can't be afraid to rely on the Holy Spirit.

Bible Verses:

*For the Lord himself will come down from heaven, with a loud command, with the voice of the archangel and with the trumpet call of God, and the dead in Christ will rise first. After that, we who are still alive and are left will be caught up together with them in the clouds to meet the Lord in the air. And so we will be with the Lord forever. Therefore encourage one another with these words.* 1 Thessalonians 4:16–18

These verses gave me hope for the future. I can't wait until the day I see my mom again.

## Chapter 24

## I Plan to Give You a Hope and a Future

## With Ruthann David

*Ruthann was seventy-two years old at the time of the interview. Her mom, Doris, died at the age of forty-nine, in 1970, when Ruthann was twenty-six years old.*

My parents died at the same time, in a plane crash, April 19, 1970. My dad was the pilot, flying another couple, who were missionaries. They went from Alma, Michigan, to Pennsylvania, for a retreat weekend. All four of them died instantly on the return trip home. At the time, I was in Kenya, East Africa, working as a missionary teacher living in the bush, and had only been there for eight months. Our parents died on a Sunday night, and the word was relayed to me through telegram and short-wave radio. When I got the news, at first, I had a weird reaction, and laughed. Then I thought I was going to faint when my friends prayed with me. I got on a plane in Nairobi the next day headed home to Michigan.

My dad agreed to fly their friends, the Rehners, to a retreat center and spend the weekend with them. My mom and dad spoke while they were at the other couple's home church. My mom even led a devotional. They had a wonderful time and thought about staying overnight, but since the weather cleared, they decided to leave. On the way back, the weather turned bad with horrible wind and rain. They tried to land in Lansing, but my dad somehow missed the airport. They crashed near home, in Fowler, on a farm field. Later we learned wind shear was likely the cause.

When we were children, my mom always tried to make everything so special for all of us. She threw wonderful birthday parties for my sisters and me. When she asked what kind of cake I wanted, I usually requested an angel food cake with crushed up pistachios, to which she added frosting and whipped cream on the top. Christmas was always a very big deal at our house, when we were growing up, with memorable traditions. We styled our hair and paraded down the stairs, while my dad took movies of us. We'd sit around in our pajamas for the morning. She was such a great cook and even liked to try different things for the holidays, such as lobster tail one year.

My mom had such a devout faith and had a real heart for prayer. One of my favorite memories as a child was when she read stories to us. Mom was a big reader and read more than just fun fiction like I do. She read devotional, Christian living, the Bible, and even theological books. She was a deep thinker, was in the National Honor Society, and should have gone to college but never did.

My mom could listen to people like they were the only people in the room. I don't feel I do this nearly as well as she did, but I try. She was so kind to others. I desire more faith to remember God is in control of my life, that He's going to guide me, and He will give me answers. My mom had that kind of faith.

She and dad were around the first time I dated Ray, my husband now. One time, when he broke up with me, I was moping around, and my mom set me in front of the sewing machine and said, "Here!" My sister was getting married that summer, and I wasn't, although I was the oldest. I cried and cried, as I sewed pearls on her wedding dress. It was good for me to do that because I had to learn to love others and be happy for them.

My mom taught me so many things. We loved to do simple things such as washing the dishes together, talking the whole time. Also, I did my mom's hair. I'd comb it out and put it up in rollers for her. The first time I went to Kenya, my mom and I were up until 3 a.m. the night before I left, talking. We talked about what I would take, about writing one another, and countless other things. It was the last time I talked with her one on one. We didn't have television, phone, or electricity in Kenya. I still have some of the letters we wrote to each other.

When my parents died, my second sister, Pat, was three and a half months pregnant, and my youngest sister, Suzanne, was staying with her for the weekend. They were wondering why it took so long for our parents to get back. The state police arrived at their house at the same time as our pastor, to tell them what happened.

It was so sudden. We had no preparation. When I got home on Thursday afternoon, I went straight to the visitation. Although they had to do a closed casket because of the plane crash, that's the first time it seemed real. Coming home so quickly and flying so far left me in a daze.

You'd think after all these years, I'd be able to talk about my mom without crying, but I can't. So many people came to the visitations, even one of the professors from Anderson College, where I attended, came for me. Many people I grew up with in the community, school, and church were in attendance. Alma is a close-knit town of around ten thousand people.

My two oldest sisters and I went back to our parents' house after the visitation and talked far into the night. I sat down at the piano and played, "It Is Well with My Soul," and of course all of us ended up crying, but it was a healing time for us. We didn't stay overnight there because it didn't seem like home anymore now that they were gone. When we finally went back to our sister's house, we went through letters and cards, and reminisced. My youngest sister Suzanne didn't want to talk with us. Talking about our parents made her upset and she'd leave the room. She was the only one who was still living with my parents. Suddenly, both of them were gone, so I think it was the hardest for her, being only thirteen years old. Carolyn was twenty-one, Pat was twenty-three, and I was twenty-six.

It was estimated that around five hundred people came to the funeral, leaving some standing. We sat our youngest sister between us in the front row. My grandmother on my mom's side, grandparents on my dad's side, and aunts and uncles encircled us through the whole thing. The support

I felt from our church family meant so much to us. My parents were prominent and active in our church. My mom was a Sunday school teacher and church librarian. The choir performed, a friend sang a solo, and we all sang songs they liked. It was a touching and precious service.

After a couple months, I went back to Kenya, but I often wonder if it was a good decision. My sister Suzanne calls me her second mom, and she wished I had stayed home from Kenya while she was young. Sometimes I regret my decision and think I should have stayed to help her.

If my parents had been around, I think I would have stayed closer to home more. Even though I went to a few places, I am a homebody at heart. I loved the travel but couldn't wait to get home each time. It was good that I went back to Kenya because my friends helped me. I might have been more bitter about it all. I lived with nurses or teacher friends who were good to me. An older lady I lived with in Kenya had met my parents in the states. I was in college, but she was in our home for a day when she was on sabbatical and came to our church. It's neat how God orchestrated those details.

When I came home after two more years in Africa, my sister, Carolyn, and I ended up at the laundromat on Christmas Eve. It made me so sad, but we did spend Christmas day at Pat's house. Suzanne continued to live with Pat through high school. Carolyn and I couldn't stay in our parents' home with her, because neither of us had an income and wouldn't be able to pay for living expenses.

I had some people who were somewhat like mentors to me after my parents' death. A couple, who were friends with my parents stood in here and there. Also, a missionary lady in Kenya was so kind. We would bake together, and I went on a hunting trip with them. I previously knew a lot of the teachers at the school in Kenya before we went to Africa, so we attended activities together.

There are the little things I miss, like when I cook something, I can't ask my mom about it. I have a lot of her recipes, but I wish we had more time to do it together. It seems like such an insignificant thing, but I wish I could learn more from her.

When we cleaned out the family home, we all sat down for a week, sorting everything. I've kept some special things that were my mom's, such as a buffalo horn thimble case that was carried across the prairie on a Conestoga wagon by my great-great-great-grandma, and has passed down through many generations. I have a lacy hankie of my mom's that I carried in my wedding, and a necklace that was hers. My sister, Pat, is the memorabilia collector in the family, and she kept newspaper clippings, cards, letters, and death certificates.

I went to BSF (Bible Study Fellowship) this year, and we studied the book of Revelation. It reminded me that I will see my mom again. I believe I will know my parents, and that always gives me hope. My mom taught us from the time we were very young that God loves us. I pray to pass it on to others and my stepchildren too. When I'm out and about driving or walking, I'm able to have communion with the Lord. Even when I have difficulties, I know He's with me.

Something I'd like to do is visit the site of the plane crash because I've never been back there. The children of the couple who was in the crash with my parents would like to go there with us. It's just a field, but I think it will be interesting and healing to do that. We reunited with the Rehners in 2016, and I would like to continue to meet with them. My sisters live close by the cemetery where my parents are buried and are good about putting flowers on their gravesite. My visits to the cemetery are much less frequent. My sisters and I call one another each year on the date of the accident. We are intentional about getting together to keep the family ties strong. Through the years, many times, my sisters and I prayed together. I'm so thankful our parents taught us to do that because it was a lifeline for me. We often had tears, but I feel that tears can be healing.

Sometimes, I've been able to help others by just being a comfort and letting them talk when they are grieving. After dating when young, Ray and I had no contact for many years. I remained single until I was fifty-three years old. When my husband's mom died, he called to tell me, and I went to the funeral. We shared a common loss. We began a relationship again, and soon got married. It's interesting that while I was in college, I was dating Ray, and he and my parents knew each other. I'm not a mother, but I love children. Now, I have eleven grandchildren through my husband. It's amazing God planned for this to happen.

A daughter carries so much more of her mom within herself than she realizes. Be kind to people because you never know if they are visiting angels. Sometimes, a memory pops up here or there. I don't know if it was a dream or a vision, but each of us sisters, individually, felt they had one of our parents come to visit us after their death.

My experience was with my dad, but he came to me and said everything will be okay. They were both happy. That fills me with joy. I look forward to seeing my mom in heaven.

Bible Verses:

*"For I know the plans I have for you," declares the LORD, "plans to prosper you and not to harm you, plans to give you a hope and a future."* Jeremiah 29:11

*For I am the LORD your God who takes hold of your right hand and says to you, Do not fear; I will help you.* Isaiah 41:13

## Chapter 25

## Nothing Can Separate Us

## With Judy Boeve

*Judy was forty-seven at the time of the interview. Judy's mom, Angeline, died at the age of sixty-six, on June 6, 1990, when Judy was twenty-one years old.*

I pulled open the huge white door leading into our country church's sanctuary, on that first Sunday after my mom died. So many flower arrangements had been sent for my mom's funeral that previous week, that they overflowed from the pulpit area to fill every seat of the choir loft behind it. The sight and scent overwhelmed me.

When I was a little girl, when my mom, and older sister, Joan, were working on a sewing project, they'd create a little project for me to do with them. In later years, I took 4-H to learn sewing, but I really missed my mom because she couldn't help me. If I got frustrated during sewing class, the instructor would say, "Go back and read the instructions." There wasn't a book of instructions to help me when my mom got Alzheimer's disease.

Piano music often filled our home when I was growing up. My mom played even many years past the onset of the disease. She taught me how to cook and bake, and I enjoy those activities now. We were a simple farming family, and our treasure didn't lie with money. We went on a few vacations to visit relatives. It was important to my parents to spend quality time with immediate and extended family.

My kids only knew the grandparents on my husband's side. I missed my parents when my kids had events like Grandparent's Day at school. They weren't around when I had my kids, just as my mom didn't have her parents when I was born. There's a disconnect or a void for me, not to have parents, but my kids never had maternal grandparents, so they didn't know the difference.

When I was around twelve years old, I had an experience which was a turning point. Sometime after my mom's diagnosis, I went to her during the night. She wouldn't wake up to comfort me. She would normally say, "Come on, come sleep by me." This night she didn't respond, and I knew I would never have that part of her again. I was terribly upset and cried at the realization of that. The attentive, caring mom of my childhood was not going to help me from now on. It was like it was the beginning of her death. I didn't cry about anything else for years, especially concerning my mom, her disease, or her lack of attention for me.

My dad took care of her at home, even though he had the beginnings of Parkinson's disease. He considered it his responsibility and cared for her from his heart until she died. God gave him extra strength. Her disease was a slow process over nine years. The systems in her body forgot how to work correctly and slowly shut down. I felt stuck there at home, being the youngest by many years behind my siblings. I observed my dad's commitment and sometimes felt guilty for being so immature and selfish in my teenage years.

I knew Jesus since I was very young. We were brought up with prayers and Bible reading, going to church, and Christian activities. But when I was sixteen, I went on a mission trip that changed my life. I went down to Atlanta with a group of teenagers and leaders, and while there I had experiences that brought me closer to the Lord. I felt the Holy Spirit working in the Bible school we led and also in the worship and communion services we had. I sensed the presence of the Lord strongly and never was the same after that trip.

My mom had a strong Christian faith and was a spiritual leader at home until she got too sick. Earlier on, she was the one to spur us on to do our catechism lessons, read the Bible, and pray. Later, my dad was in that position, and he was the full-time caretaker for my mom. Since I was about thirteen years old, my sister Joan and I helped with my mom's bathing, and did a lot of the weekly cooking and baking.

In my teenage years, my mom and I had distance, so I couldn't relate to moms and daughters who had closeness. When I was in Dutch dance as a teenager, and a mother brushed a teenage daughter's hair, I remember almost mocking it. I think I must have been jealous of the other girls. Until I had my own teenage daughter, I couldn't understand it. Most of my friends still had their parents, and I was frustrated as a teen, because they didn't fully understand my situation. At Mother-Daughter banquets at church, Marcia, my sister-in-law, would always make sure I sat with her and her mom.

I often wondered what my mom would have said about dating. My sister, Joan, who is fifteen years older, helped me when she could. She gave advice, such as, "Keep asking him questions." She thought I should ask my dates questions to get to know them. My mom could help Joan with her wedding, and of course, I would have loved her to help with mine. My sister Joan was a mentor to me, and we are very close to this day. My sister-in-law Marcia, and my other sisters-in-law are helpful and special to me.

I'd like to ask my mom about everyday things, like cooking and baking. Since my mom was such a great cook, I have a lot of experience. She took great joy in cooking for others, and now I also have the heart to share meals with families who need them, and do so whenever possible.

Since my mom was losing her abilities, she would do embarrassing things at times, such as making a mess at meals or singing inappropriately at church. I knew she couldn't help it, but it was hard for me to see her act that way. When I left for college, it was so thoughtful of church friends to take turns sitting in the church basement with my mom, so my dad could go to the church service upstairs.

After my mom died, our pastor asked me if there was anything special we wanted him to say about my mom at the funeral. I had a great memory to share. When I went to college, my mom would ask my dad over and over, "Is Judy coming back for supper?" She still knew who I was. One time, when I visited my mom, something significant happened. She could still look at me, write answers to me, and was wearing her glasses, but she could no longer speak. I wasn't mean or sassy anymore; I had more patience and maturity.

I wrote her questions, and she could write something back. I asked her about her family, and she answered, "My parents." I said, "Your mom and dad are dead." I thought, *Doesn't she realize this?* She stared at me with a frightened look. I thought, *Oh, in her mind, she thought they were still alive.* I asked the question, "Who makes you beautiful?" The first time, she said, "Raymond," my dad's name. I don't know why I kept asking that question. It must have been God prompting me to get her answer. I asked her again, and she wrote, "The spiritual creature," the first time correctly. Then she wrote it a second time with mixed up letters. When she seemed frustrated, I finally stopped asking her.

Later I asked my dad what she might have been talking about. He said, "She means the Holy Spirit." I was amazed that my mom had a closeness to the Holy Spirit, when she couldn't talk, didn't know her parents weren't alive, and didn't know my brothers and sisters anymore. The Holy Spirit will never leave us or forsake us, nothing can separate us from the love of God. He will not leave you if you can't think straight, or get Alzheimer's! I wish I still had that paper she wrote on. She was combining scripture and spiritual thoughts on the paper. This is the memory the pastor shared at her funeral, about her closeness to the Holy Spirit.

In her last months, my mom wasn't responding much anymore and was very quiet. I was going to get married, and I wanted her to be at my wedding. She was my mom! I decided that if she were living, she would be there. It wasn't a choice I would need to make, because a few weeks before our wedding, she was obviously very sick and close to death.

Her body organs were shutting down, and hospice came to our house the last week to help out. On my mom's last day, the nurse said she wouldn't make it through the night. I spent a few moments with her the night before she died. As I rubbed her arm, she looked at me. She could no longer talk or move any muscles. Then I walked out. She was gone the next morning.

I felt bad that my siblings knew her through their young adult years, and they would always know her better. I missed out on her! By the time I was about twelve, she began going downhill, so I felt cheated. I had just turned twenty-one, and my siblings were all in their thirties and forties when she passed away.

It was a long week! She died on Wednesday, and the funeral was on Saturday. We had two evenings of visitation, which was so tiring. It was nice that so many people came—the neighbors, friends from church, and farmers who were finished planting their fields. My husband-to-be, Steve, stuck with me for five years, and saw my mom decline. I know I was immature and had a difficult time dealing with everything.

One of my neighbors came through the visitation, and obviously he knew we were getting married. He said, "She didn't quite make it, did she?" I broke down crying, and he immediately felt awful, but I know he was just trying to be caring. I was so full of emotions. *We were so close to my wedding! Just three more weeks*! I asked God, "Why, why, why?" A depressing thing was that she was buried in the beautiful blue dress she would have worn at my wedding.

I forced myself to go to our church the Sunday after the funeral. I didn't want the first time I came into that sanctuary after my mom's funeral, to be my wedding day. Most of the flowers were still up front. They had a candle on the piano in honor of my mom.

Way before she died, I had accepted that my mom was gone, but I still had to go through the stages of grief. I just wanted to get through my wedding first. I declared, "We're having a wedding!"

On my wedding day, I went upstairs in the balcony before our pictures began, to be by myself. My flowers for my wedding were abundant and so beautiful. I looked at the flowers and thought to myself, *I can't compete with how many flowers were up there for my mom, but there are a lot of them, and they're all for me. Just for me. This is nice.* During our ceremony, the minister mentioned, "You're probably thinking about mom." I think I shook my head, no. I wasn't thinking about her except the flower issue beforehand. I was self-centered and had a hard time processing all that had happened.

Hospice gave us a book that was about the grieving process, called, *Living when a Loved One Has Died*. It helped my dad as we went through it together, and later I reread it. I liked it so much, that I have given copies to other people over the years when a loved one passed away.

After my dad died years later, we finished splitting up all of our mom's possessions. I got her cedar chest and the things inside, which included her wedding dress and a beaded veil. When my husband and I were expecting our first child, the nurse at the doctor's office said to me, "Oh, you can tell your mom!" I thought, *No, she has passed away.* After difficult years, we experienced the birth of our first child. Now, we are so blessed to have a daughter and a son!

If I had a chance, I would ask my mom, "What do you think about how I've raised my kids?" I might ask her if she's proud of me.

My greatest hope is the return of Jesus. When He left earth to go back up to heaven, the angels asked the witnesses, "What are you looking at? He will return in the same way he left." There are promises in the Bible, and heaven is a very real place, way beyond our comprehension. There will be no more sickness, crying, or death. Mom's already there, and I'm looking forward to being there someday.

I had faith, even in the awful times, knowing it wasn't the end. You can have joy, even when you're not happy, knowing inner peace for the future. I don't know how people go through this without the promise of heaven. You couldn't say goodbye for a little bit of time, you would be saying goodbye forever. I have more empathy now when I go to a funeral visitation. I don't usually say much, but if I do, I say something like, "Moms are the most special people in the world." Or I use the present tense, like, "She is a wonderful person."

It's strange how when I was losing my mom, most of my friends could not relate, as we were all so young. Now the parents of my friends are becoming elderly, and I can't relate as much, because my parents have been gone for so many years.

What I can say to others is that it is not easy. It's heart wrenching. You lose a piece of yourself when you lose your mom, but with God, He gives you a peace that's bigger than the situation. He's bigger than death, and He promises we'll all be together again.

This all confirms in my mind how real God is. I will die someday. I want to be a great mom to my kids, especially since my son is still young. I pray God will let me help him and be his mom longer. God loves us even when we go through hard things and don't feel His love. God reminds me that He is in charge. When my husband, Steve, was diagnosed with cancer, I didn't know how to process that. Thankfully his health is now restored. Our prayers can make a difference; we have to keep praying. I don't know how it all works, but sometimes His answer is yes, and sometimes no. I have to stay close to God, the best I can. One day we won't have these imperfect bodies. In heaven we'll have perfect bodies. That's the hope of God.

Bible Verses:

*For I am persuaded that neither death nor life, nor angels nor principalities nor powers, nor things present nor things to come, nor height nor depth, nor any other created thing, shall be able to separate us from the love of God which is in Christ Jesus our Lord.* Romans 8:38–39 NKJV

She was allowed to get Alzheimer's. I get so angry with Satan for making sin and sickness in the world. He took my mother away! But the love of God provides so we will see one another again in heaven.

*For the Lord himself will descend from heaven with a cry of command, with the voice of an archangel, and with the sound of the trumpet of God. And the dead in Christ will rise first. Then we who are alive, who are left, will be caught up together with them in the clouds to meet the Lord in the air, and so we will always be with the Lord. Therefore encourage one another with these words.* 1 Thessalonians 4:16–18 ESV

My dad used to remind us, "The trump will sound!"

*And we know that in all things God works for the good of those who love him, who have been called according to his purpose.* Romans 8:28

This is my favorite verse in the Bible.

Myrna Folkert

# IN THEIR THIRTIES WHEN MOM DIED

# Chapter 26

## I'm Going to See Jesus

## With Rachel Brink

*Rachel's age at the time of the interview was thirty-three. Her mom, Karen, died at the age of fifty-seven, on January 10, 2014, when Rachel was thirty-one.*

The summer before my mom was going into her thirtieth year of teaching, we noticed she was acting strange. She was usually very organized and on top of everything, but she began to forget things, was paranoid, seemed confused, and said things that didn't make sense. My dad didn't think much of it and thought she should start the year and see how it would go.

She was a phenomenal teacher. She moved up one grade from young fives to kindergarten, and all twenty-five of her students' parents requested to have her for a second year because they loved her. She began the year, but she was so frustrated, came home weeping a lot, and was upset with herself. We wondered if it was menopause, thyroid, or hormones, as we heard those can greatly affect a woman her age.

She continued to try to teach that first semester in the fall of 2012. Things didn't go well, and she had to take early retirement by the middle of October. My dad was a teacher and football coach at a different school district, and he continued teaching that year. My mom was getting to the point she needed 24-hour care, so fortunately I could arrange my busy schedule to assist her.

My mom was the prime example of the Christian faith. When we were growing up, every morning before my brother Nate and I went to school, she was at the table doing her devotions. She wrote and journaled a lot. I have her Bible and journals. She struggled with self-esteem and depression. I saw my mom hold her feelings in and abuse herself internally. She also worked too hard and too many hours when teaching. She was so loving, giving, and caring, but everyone has flaws. My mom's legacy is that she loved in her actions, touching so many people and so many children at school. I'd like to talk to her about how to be a better wife and how to live out my faith in my life, like she did.

I miss the daily stuff with my mom, like going to Target, baking together, and doing things for other people. We shared intimately with each other, and we shopped and traveled. We made trips to Iowa, where her sister lived, we did a lot of walking together, and since I'm a big runner, I convinced her to do her first 5K run.

My mom and I were always close and talked every day, even when I went to college in Iowa. Despite not having cell phones and being many miles away from each other we still managed to talk multiple times daily. During college, I had issues with self-esteem too. My mom thought it was her fault and took on a lot of blame for me getting sick with an eating disorder. Our relationship was strained for a couple years.

We went to many doctor appointments during her last years, attempting to find what was going on with her and try to rule things out. She was progressively getting worse. Finally, by Christmas, she got a diagnosis at U of M, of frontotemporal dementia when she was only fifty-five years old. By that time, there was nothing we could do. They said it was too late for medication. You could see the deterioration of her brain on the scans.

In a way, we lost her a year before her actual death. She was healthy in other ways, but not her brain. People confuse her disease with Alzheimer's disease. Frontotemporal dementia is different, although it looks somewhat the same. It scares me, because my mom's mom had Alzheimer's, but later in life. We donated Mom's brain to Harvard after she died, so they could study it, but we haven't heard anything. She was a unique case because she was young and active, and it was so strange how it happened.

During most of the year of 2013, I took care of her. I had to take time off from my job as a social worker for Love In the Name of Christ, a mission that partners with local churches. Although it was hard, I don't regret one minute I cared for her, and I would do it all over again. Sometimes she would drive the car, but she began to be a danger to herself and others, so we finally had to take the keys away for good. She also walked away from her daycare and got lost. We tried having her at a couple facilities, but nothing worked out.

She got worse. No facility would take her anymore because she was young, and they thought she could escape. Finally, my dad realized she couldn't be alone and stayed home the following school year, in the fall of 2013. He was convinced he could still take care of her and kept her home much longer than I think he should have. She ended up getting into Freedom Inn in the fall. She was declining by the week.

When she was in the nursing facility, I didn't handle it well. I thought, *Why am I visiting my mom at a nursing home? It's not supposed to be this way.* I went every day, and sometimes even a couple times a day. I wanted to have every possible moment with her, lay in bed with her, just be there. It was hard on my marriage because I was gone all the time and under so much stress. She could recognize me and said, "Rachee." When my mom was sick, and I couldn't control what was happening to her, I reverted back some and didn't take care of myself.

Finally, we had hospice come in. She couldn't talk the last few weeks. The hardest part of her disease, for me, was the anger she displayed. It was so unlike her. She couldn't verbalize her feelings, and it was like her mind was trapped. They used to call this disease Lewy body dementia.

At first I didn't understand how the disease would kill her, but then I watched it slowly happen when her systems and organs began to shut down. My birthday is January 7, and we were counting down the hours, hoping it wouldn't happen on my birthday. Her last words were a few days before she died. When I was leaving her room, she said to me, "It's okay, I'm going to see Jesus." She knew it and I knew it, but I still couldn't let it happen and let her go.

On the last couple of days, the whole family was gathered around her as she was breathing terribly loud. My dad kept telling her, "Thank you, thank you, for all you did for me." We were all getting so worn out because she kept hanging on day after day. One evening, my dad stayed. My brother and I left to go home. I didn't know if I wanted to see her take her last breath or not. There had been so many goodbyes already. I believe my mom knew it would be too hard on me to see it. She made it until January 10, but my birthday has never been the same. Five minutes after I got home, I got a call from my dad that she had passed away, but I didn't go back to see her.

She hadn't looked like herself for the last few months. I didn't see her again until the funeral visitation. I was adamant about not having an open casket because she looked so much different. But the mortician had a photograph of her at my wedding, and he did a great job with her, so we agreed to have viewing.

The visitations were lengthy and tiring. Many teachers, and past students came. Some were teens or young adults whom she taught in kindergarten. They said things like, "I had your mom," or "She was the best teacher I ever had!" We were blessed by the stories they told. The weather was horrible that January of 2014, so that prevented some friends from coming.

At the funeral, we sang "How Great Thou Art." Her two best teacher friends spoke, my brother, who is also a pastor, spoke, and my dad's best friend said words on behalf of my dad. I knew I wanted to speak, to honor her, but when I stood up and looked at my dad, he was crying his eyes out. They had been married over thirty-five years. It was so hard to see him cry. He usually has a very hard time expressing his emotions.

At the funeral, I read something I wrote:

*"For years I have been raging against the dementia that was slowly devouring my mother's life, her very self. I will never fully grieve the loss of the woman my mother once was—the strong, thoughtful woman who generously shared her wisdom, strength, and recipes, encouraged my career, and took delight in taking me shopping to Target on any given day. My mom's spirit will live within me each and every moment. I will try to take*

*care of myself because I know that is what she would want. She gave her everything to me, and I will try to carry on her legacy."*

The worst part for me was when they took the casket away at the end of the funeral. I can still see it. We didn't have a burial; we had her cremated.

For the funeral lunch, I asked some friends to prepare her famous Peanut Butter Ritz cookies she used to make for others. It was her special touch at the funeral. She loved to cook and bake for people. Now, I have a home business, making meals and other baked goods.

My mom's best friend is now my mentor, and she calls me her daughter. I've always known her, and now we're best friends. It's a very special relationship, which is amazing and genuine. I call Ellen, Mom, and her husband, Dad. Two other friends of my mom's are also my very close friends of mine. I don't have many girlfriends around my own age. I'm blessed, and thankful for all the wonderful women in my life who support me like my mom did.

I kind of lost my dad too. He began dating a month after my mom died. When he asked me what I thought, I told him, "I can't tell you what to do, but it would be really hard if you married again." The first year after my mom died, when it was a holiday or birthday, my dad was already remarried, so it was awkward to mention my mom. I wanted my dad to be happy, but it was way too much, way too fast for me. In that period of your life when you become a young adult, your mom becomes your best friend. My dad and I became very close during my mom's illness, but since he remarried, there has been emotional distance between us.

I'm thankful I have a lot of items from my mom, such as many journals and lots of photographs. She expressed feelings in her journals that she couldn't express out loud. I have all the letters she sent me in college. The journals talk about her depression and struggle that she never shared with us verbally. I had her wedding diamond made into a necklace. The funeral director told us about *Thummies*. They are Mom's thumbprint and her birthstone set together and put on a necklace. I usually wear mine, and rub it, because it makes me feel close to her.

After a time, I began to ask my dad about burying Mom. She was cremated, and Dad had the urn. After my mom passed away, I sat down by the Window on the Waterfront, a park in our city, and cried because I wanted to be able to go to a cemetery where I could at least honor her. I needed some closure to help me with my grieving. My dad avoided it for a long time, and I had to do the paperwork and really push him. After quite a bit of stress and family tension, we finally had a nice service at the cemetery and buried her urn with her ashes, in the spring of 2016.

The biggest thing my mom taught me is to appreciate my body just the way it is. My mom always wanted me to take care of myself. In the profession I have, a social worker, you have to take care of yourself before you can take care of others. Now I'm back to practicing healthy coping mechanisms.

I know I will see my mom again, happy and full of life. There are times I want to leave this earth now and go to heaven because I want to see my mom. But there's a reason I'm still here, and until then, I will live it out.

I've told the girls in the youth group at my church these kinds of things. When I'm around friends younger than me, I tell them to spend every possible moment with their moms. Sometimes they say, "I hate my mom." I hope they appreciate their mom for everything she does for them. They're so lucky to have her. I tell the girls, love your mom, and tell her you love her every day. When you're angry or sad, don't take her for granted because tomorrow she could be gone.

The death of my mom changed every part of me. How could it not? There's never a moment of the day when I don't think of her. My mom was the cornerstone of the traditions and keeping our family together. Now we're no longer close. For a long time, I tried to be in her position of holding our family together, but it has not worked out.

It's been therapeutic to talk about my mom. It's good to talk about the memories and the good things, and the legacy she lived. It makes me miss her, but I feel better knowing that I'm going to be okay. She's in a better place now. I often question why God would take her away from me so young. But it's for a reason, and He has put other people in my life to help me.

Because of the population I work with, in social work, I hear so many awful stories that put my life in perspective. Some people never had a mom or had terrible situations, and I was blessed to have my mom for thirty-one years.

I like this saying from an anonymous author. "My mom taught me everything except how to live without her."

Bible verses:

*Wait on the LORD; be of good courage, and He shall strengthen your heart.* Psalm 27:14 NKJV

*She is clothed in strength and dignity, and she laughs without fear of the future.* Proverbs 31:25 NLT

«Chapter 27

Run to God

With Janice Broyles

*Janice was thirty-seven when her mom, Sharon, died at the age of sixty-five, on October 10, 2012. At the time of the interview, Janice was forty years old.*

We were not aware of my mom having any type of heart related problems. She was a diabetic and had high blood pressure, but those were under control. She was eating right, exercising, and active.

What we pieced together about her death is that she suffered a heart attack. In her attempt to get help, she fell and hit her head on the nightstand. We don't know what happened first: the heart attack or hitting her head. I found her lying on the floor next to her bed, face first in a pool of urine on the carpet. Afterward, they determined she had a minor heart attack and then died of asphyxiation. It all came as such a shock, and we didn't know she was at risk for a heart attack to occur. She had brain damage because of lying face down on the carpet for so long.

My mother and I talked on Tuesday afternoon. When I came home from work on Wednesday afternoon, mom's coworker called because she didn't show up for her volunteer job. It was strange because my mom was always very organized and dependable. When she said she was going to do something, you could count on it. That kind of thing never happened with my mom.

She lived with us, but had her own private apartment above our garage. When I looked up there, the only light was the little stove light she kept on when she went to bed each night. I knew something was off. I looked in the garage, and her car was there. That's when I panicked.

Sometimes she needed a shot of insulin or something. The strong, pungent smell of urine hit me when I opened the door to go upstairs to her apartment. My heart dropped to my feet, and I ran up the stairs to her side. The urine-soaked the mattress and carpet all around her, but she was still alive. I called and waited for an ambulance. I regretted not finding my mom earlier. I thought, *If only I could have one more chance.* Never will I forget the smell at the bottom of the stairs.

It was estimated she was in that position for about sixteen hours. Guilt consumed me for not knowing. A gut-wrenching feeling that what happened to her was irreversible, tied my stomach in knots. That was the beginning of a whirlwind week, as my siblings flew into town. After my mom was in the hospital five days, they began to discover she had brain damage from the fall or the asphyxiation.

We waited by her side for a week, hoping she would wake up from her coma. I thought I might need to put her in a residential care facility. Finally, after discussing things with her doctors, I made the hard decision to let her go. My siblings all had differing opinions about what should happen, but I had custody of her and had to make the final call.

The Lord gave me peace about everything. My mom wouldn't want to hang on, unable to do anything. She said to me, "When it's my time to go, then let me go." During the week in the hospital, most of my siblings thought she might pull through. They didn't want to believe she was going to die.

I prayed, "Lord, if it's her time to go, please take her. If it's Your will, then please don't let her suffer." We pulled the plug, which simply meant they no longer gave her drugs to prolong her life. Because I knew this is what she wanted, there wasn't much remorse. My biggest fear was that she would starve to death, but of course, that's not what happens. We then put her into hospice care.

It was a gray, rainy October evening when she went into the hospice house. I left for the night, and went to work in the morning. Shortly after I got to work the next morning, my brother and sister-in-law called when she had taken her last breath. We had said our goodbyes. I was glad she didn't have to suffer anymore. She passed away only twelve hours after she arrived at the hospice house.

There were many major decisions I had to make, like whether to cremate her or bury her. She didn't have any money to fight over. There were some decisions I made that my siblings were not happy with, but when it was all over, we were at peace with one another.

We had two memorial services for her, which were very nice. I didn't have time to grieve at the beginning. I had to make plans and all the business details. I had to keep myself together. By operating on autopilot making these decisions, I didn't think about the emotional part at that time. The Lord was my rock during the entire process and kept me standing.

I was very blessed to be brought up in a God honoring home. My mom had a strong belief in the Lord. My parents belonged to the Pentecostal denomination. My best memory of my mom is when she danced and sang in church. When the choir would start *a-singin' and a clappin'*, my mom would feel the Spirit. It was quite a sight to see!

When a loved one dies, I believe people do one of two things: they either run away from God or they run to God. Thank the Lord for His peace and presence—I especially felt Him with me the first night in the hospital with my mom, before my siblings arrived.

At first, I held it together, and it didn't hit me that Mom was gone. One night, two weeks after her death, everything hit me. When I was alone in bed, I sobbed and did not stop for hours. I could finally let all my emotions out.

Mom and I were very close and talked about everything. I miss her every day. I am thankful I have some special possessions from her, such as her Bible, her devotional journal, and some blankets she crocheted or quilted. There are times when I'm gardening, and I want to call her. Ben, my son, got baptized this September, and I wished she were there. Because of my mom's influence, I'm a better mother. I let my boys know how much I love them, just in case. Not having a maternal grandma around anymore affected my seventeen-year-old, Jonathon, more so than my seven-year-old, Benjamin. Jonathon will often say, "I miss Grandma."

My mom taught me how to love, how to pray, and how to never to give up even when life doesn't turn out the way you expect it to. If she were here today, I'd ask her what heaven is like. I'd just listen to her talk. I don't think my faith ever wavered, but it actually was solidified by the loss of my mother. I know I will make it to heaven one day, and I have a goal to take as many people with me as possible! I have hope in the Lord, with the Holy Spirit working in me.

Grief never really goes away completely. You only learn to work around it, and it's okay. Grief is a reminder of the love between you and your mother. I would never want to get rid of it. God is faithful to get us through the tough times.

Bible Verse:

*Have I not commanded thee? Be strong and of a good courage; be not afraid, neither be thou dismayed: for the LORD thy God is with thee whithersoever thou goest.* Joshua 1:9 KJV

## Chapter 28

## Wipe Every Tear

## With Michele Dekker

*Michele's age at the time of the interview was fifty-four. She was thirty-five years old when her mom, Jacqueline (Jackie), died at the age of fifty-nine, on August 19, 1996.*

One day after getting a call at work that my mom was sick, being a nurse, I had a sense it was serious. When I got off the phone, I said to a coworker, "I can't do life without my mom."

In July, she began having flu-like symptoms. She was admitted into the hospital because her blood sugar was extremely high. After spending an evening at the hospital, I had a feeling I'd get a call to return, and left my clothes lying out. I was called back early on Sunday morning. First, they thought she may have had a stroke as she was very confused and lethargic. An MRI ruled out a stroke, and it revealed that her liver enzymes were extremely elevated. She needed to be sent to Ann Arbor because all her levels were so out of whack.

Fog prevented a helicopter from flying, so they sent an airplane to Tulip City Airport in Holland, to fly her to Ann Arbor. I was trying to comprehend this was all happening within four days, because she had just watched my kids on Monday. She had been tired but felt fine.

The staff at U of M was phenomenal. They made a diagnosis of Hepatitis A, a liver disease, causing her kidneys to shut down. She was placed on a ventilator and kidney dialysis, with many fluids and tubes connected to her. Being a nurse, I blame myself for not having my mom's health checked earlier that week.

She improved somewhat in that she was awake, but she couldn't talk because of the ventilator. We communicated using eye contact, nodding, and a little chalkboard to write on. My grandma, who was then eighty-six, was there too. She said to us, "She's my daughter, I am coming." Now I get that, being a mom. My dad, sister, grandma, and I stayed in a hotel connected to the hospital.

My parents attended East Saugatuck Christian Reformed Church their whole married life, so we had many people supporting us and praying. For a short time, her numbers were going up and things seemed to be improving.

My two young sons were brought to the hospital a couple times, but my mom didn't look very good. I wondered whether to let my nine-year-old son, Michael, see her. He really wanted to, because they were close, but I thought he might be upset by the way she looked, and wanted him to wait until she was better. I kept telling him, "You know, honey, she's getting better." I regret not letting Michael see her one more time, but I had to make that decision as a mom.

We were there for over two weeks. On a Friday, she was relatively stable, so most of the family went home to rest, while I stayed with my mom. During the night I got a call from the hospital again. By Saturday night, she was really struggling. They couldn't keep her blood pressure up and she wasn't doing well, but still could respond. My mom's best lifetime friend came and told my mom, "Jackie, you need to get better." The look in my mom's eyes was, *I can't do this anymore.*

We told the doctors all along that we didn't want to be unreasonable in what we were asking them to do and to let us know when it was enough. They said, at this point, they were maxed out on medicines to keep her blood pressure up. At what point might there be brain damage because of the medicines? Even if we get her through this, what are we getting her through this to? The selfish part of me thought, *I don't care if she can't respond, I can go see her, touch her, and talk to her.* But she wouldn't want that. Your heart and your head are saying two different things.

We all agreed on letting her go, but in the back of your mind, you think maybe there could still be a miracle. She's already done way more than most people do. Later, they thought possibly she could have been diabetic and didn't know it. It compromised her immune system, enabling the Hepatitis A to spread so quickly.

I was worried about pulling the plug, that she might struggle or something. They didn't even turn the ventilator off. Soon after they stopped the medicines, she opened her eyes and looked right at us. It was like she knew. She knew where she was going. Everything just started shutting down, and her blood pressure gradually went down being off the meds, as we sat around her. It was peaceful with no struggle. In about half an hour she was gone.

That night, I had the most vivid dream or vision. My mom was right in front of me and said, "I'm good, I'm fine, don't worry." She was smiling ear to ear. It might have been my hope that it was her, but it was very real and such an assurance for me.

My mom always believed and had faith. She was brought up that way and it was very important to her. We always read the Bible and prayed at mealtimes and bedtimes. My parents were a part of Bible studies at their church or with friends. It was a comfort to know that she knew she was going to be with Jesus.

When my mom was sick, I prayed like I hadn't prayed in a very long time. I think that's often the case in a situation like that. I always believed, but then it became even more real. When you get tossed in the fire, your faith becomes a bigger part of your life again. My boys and I had counseling for a while, which was so beneficial. When you go through rough times, I feel it's very wise and comforting.

When grieving, there's an ebb and flow, being happy and laughing one moment and the next you are sobbing. I was astonished by how many people came to the visitations and the stories they told us of how my mom touched their lives. She taught elementary school for over thirty years and impacted so many. Things that make you cry initially are the good things that make you smile later. More of the tears become happy tears.

Random things can sometimes get to you a long time later. I geared up the first year after my mom died, thinking of doing the "firsts" without her. I was so busy on Mother's Day, Christmas, and birthdays that I didn't have time to think. It's when you slow down a few days later that it hits you.

My mom was my best friend, and it was an odd day if we didn't talk on the phone or in person. You even had to sit by the phone then before cordless phones. If something exciting happened, I picked up the phone to tell my mom. I can't tell you the number of times I had the phone in my hand for months after her death. Then I had to remind myself that she was in a much better place.

We had to clean out her classroom very soon after she died. We left a lot but took most of her own children's books. I also love children's books, and now read them to my own grandchildren. I can't resist buying more, just like my mom.

My mom was young, and I was young, but I was so fortunate to have her for thirty-five years. Many people don't get that much time. Some people have their mom for over sixty years but never had a relationship like we had. Would I like to have her here? Absolutely! But I'm thankful for the mom I had. My grandma stepped in somewhat for me, and we were very close. But later, when she was older, I did the things my mom would have done such as her finances. I was her caretaker until she died at the age of ninety-six.

Now that I have my own grandsons, it makes me realize how much my mom would have loved to be a great-grandma. Not much has changed in my life in twenty years but so much has changed in my sons' lives. Education was so important to her, and we've had graduations and career advancements. She would be so proud of them as they've accomplished so much in twenty years.

I'm thankful for the photos, and videos so I can hear her voice. I'm almost her age now, which is a weird feeling. I would love to sit and talk with her and ask her questions. I'd also love to have my mom around to help with some decisions and run things past her. I miss that because I really valued her opinion.

My mom made a big deal of the holidays, especially Christmas. We'd be up for hours wrapping every single thing that went into the stockings, and she bought so much that she used a big bag for each person instead of the stocking. Now I carry on that tradition.

After four years, my dad did get remarried. He asked my opinion, and I told him it would be nicer if he never got married again, but he did. After some years, his second wife got Alzheimer's, and recently passed away. I feel bad for him that he lost a second wife.

My mom and I did many things together and shared some common interests. She and I loved to garden. We loved birds. We shopped and did crafts together. She gave piano lessons and I took lessons for many years, but I took them from someone else. She didn't think it was a good idea to give me the lessons herself, which I'm sure was wise.

I have quite a few keepsakes from my mom. It might sound strange, but I have a pair of her socks. We brought a bag home from the hospital that held some of her possessions, and it smelled like her. It stayed around for many years and I would randomly open it. Every once in a while, when I pull those silly socks on, it makes me feel close to her. I have some other clothes, bookshelves full of children's books, knick-knacks, and dishes.

My mom loved to do calligraphy, and one time my dad found something she had made. She made something for my sons, Michael and Jeffrey, and never gave it to them because she felt it was ruined and set it aside. She had smudged it, but it wasn't so bad that you couldn't read it. When I read it I sobbed. It was a nice note in a book, about how my parents loved them to the moon and back. It's still a nice keepsake. This was the Christmas just before she died, and she didn't know she wasn't going to be there anymore.

My love of reading and books came from my mom. We also baked, cooked, and sewed together. She was a very tidy lady, and I learned how to keep my house clean. As a working mother, when a lot of women didn't work outside the home, she was very busy, so we participated more in things like the housework.

My hope is in eternal life, forever and ever. I often wonder how people get through the death of a loved one without faith in God. First of all, I know she's in a better place. Secondly, I will see her again. It's my selfish wish that she was here, but she's doing great in heaven.

There have been opportunities to help others at work and in other situations, because I know what it's like when you lose someone close. I make it clear that I'm available to listen if they need to talk. You learn that everyone grieves differently and it's good to give people space.

I'm sensitive to people who complain about being 60 or older. I think they should be thankful for their birthdays, because my mom will forever be 59. I think, do you want a birthday, or do you want to die? Not that we don't all complain at times, but that is one of my pet peeves.

Since my mom died, I also realize how often people complain about their mothers. One time, a coworker was complaining, after a phone call with her mom, that she had to take three hours off work to take her mom to the hospital, and said she wanted to charge her. I almost said, "Did your mom charge you when you were little, and she had to take you to the doctor?" I thought later, I so wish I had the choice of taking three hours off work to take my mom somewhere. Sometimes people are sensitive enough to say to me, "I know I shouldn't complain in front of you because you don't have your mom anymore."

When you miss your mom, be thankful for what you had, if you had a good relationship. If you didn't, try to improve on that in your own family, or with your own kids and make the next generation better.

God is always here with us. The only time I feel true peace is when I've just laid it all out before Him. When I tell the Lord, I can't do it anymore, He carries me and gives me peace.

Bible Verses:

*For I know the plans I have for you, declares the LORD, plans for welfare and not for evil, to give you a future and a hope.* Jeremiah 29:11 ESV

*Well done, good and faithful servant. You have been faithful over a little; I will set you over much. Enter into the joy of your master.* Matthew 25:23 ESV

*He will wipe away every tear from their eyes, and death shall be no more, neither shall there be mourning, nor crying, nor pain anymore.* Revelation 21:4 ESV

I picture her in my mind, in the dream I had . . . the illness was all gone. She's no longer suffering. I need to remember that.

*Do not be anxious about anything, but in everything by prayer and supplication with thanksgiving let you requests be made known to God. And the peace of God, which surpasses all understanding, will guard your hearts and your minds in Christ Jesus.* Philippians 4:6-7 ESV

*Let not your hearts be troubled. Believe in God; believe also in me. In my Father's house are many rooms. If it were not so, would I have told you that I go to prepare a place for you? And if I go to prepare a place for you, I will come again and will take you to myself, that where I am you may be also.* John 14:1–3 ESV

*Be strong and let your heart take courage, all you who wait for the LORD!* Psalm 31:24 ESV

*They who wait for the LORD shall renew their strength; they shall mount up with wings like eagles; they shall run and not be weary; they shall walk and not faint.* Isaiah 40:31 ESV

# Chapter 29

# Without Faith, It Would Be Hopeless

# With Joy Meyer

*Joy was fifty-two at the time of the interview. Her mom, Ruth, was sixty-five years old at her death on September 23, 1994, when Joy was thirty years old.*

The day my mom died; we had been at my parent's house all evening. She was hanging on with heavy breathing. We left around 11 p.m. My family said they'd call us if anything happened. We got a call from one of my brothers at 2 a.m. that she had passed away. She surpassed the six months the doctors had predicted and lived about eight months. We went back and waited around for the funeral home attendants to come and take her body.

I'm thankful I was brought up in a Christian home where it was natural to learn about Jesus daily. I knew having Jesus in my heart was something I wanted in my life. My mom's faith was strong.

I didn't grow up with grandmothers around. My dad's mom, Grandma K., passed away before I was born. Grandma B., who was my mom's mom, died when I was a young adult. They were the stoic Dutch types—they didn't talk or play with you when you went to their house but sat in their chairs. They had one box of toys to play with, and you had to sit quietly on the floor.

My mom loved to cook, but when I tried to help her as a child, I felt like I was in the way. Somehow, I got some of her cooking and baking skills because people say I'm a great cook. She had a green thumb for gardening. I like it, but I'm not very successful at it. We took trips when I was young. The last one was when I was a senior in high school, and my brothers were all married. I went with my mom and dad to Alberta, Canada. When I was younger, we often went up north, or to family camp at Camp Geneva.

Just the way my mom lived, was a witness. She always had her Bible around, and I know she did devotional time much more faithfully than I do. I know she prayed for all of the kids and grandkids. She didn't have a job outside the home, and she watched my kids or the other grandkids quite often. She treated people well. My mom liked to have people over, and they had Bible studies at their house, or people stayed there from out of town.

My mom was diagnosed with liver cancer, in January of 1994. At that time, I had three children under the age of seven and was pregnant with our fourth one. I was so busy at the time and my two sisters-in-law, who are nurses, took over the responsibilities of the doctor appointments and much of my mom's care. I had our fourth child just before my mom died. She lived long enough to see my daughter baptized.

She did some chemotherapy and felt better during the summer until the first of September. At the end of the summer they decided to end treatment because she had many side effects and wanted to enjoy the time she had left. After Labor Day, she went downhill fast. My second son's birthday is September 14, so we brought the party and cake to her bedside that night. That's the last time she was fairly coherent. She died on the 23rd of September.

At the funeral visitation, everyone kept talking about what a special lady she was. The fact that so many people came to her visitation showed that many loved her. There weren't hurtful comments, but I felt like I didn't know her very well. We got along, but we didn't talk deeply because we were both quiet people. When I look back, I wish we had been closer. My parents went to a different church than us, and we didn't see one another as much as when we attended the same church. She and I talked on the phone and in person, but not about personal things. I'm not mad at her, but there was some kind of disconnect between us.

At the funeral, they sang "It Is Well with My Soul." It was a favorite of my mom's. It was held at the chapel of the funeral home, not at church. We rode to the cemetery in Overisel, Michigan, where I was brought up, for her burial service.

I don't know how someone would get through a death like this if they didn't know the Lord. It was wonderful knowing that so many people were praying for us. I had to keep going for my big family. You don't have time to sit and think about it.

The death of my mom affected the way I mother my own children. I think it still affects me today, in that I'm careful and thoughtful. My kids weren't without a grandma long because my dad married Joey in 1996, two years later. She was always Grandma to my kids because they were so young when my mom died. My oldest was seven when my mom passed away, and my youngest was born just before she died. The children of my siblings, their cousins, knew my mom as Grandma more. They had different grandmas.

Joey and I weren't close about deeply personal things, but I felt like she was there for me. She was somewhat of a mentor for me. I miss her too. It's only been a short time since she died. She was a very kind and loving person. She stepped in the best she could. I think I'm a bit guarded and don't let people get close to me. I don't enjoy talking on the phone; I email with a best friend.

There have been several times when I wished my mom was here with me. I dealt with breast cancer after she was gone. I had a partial hysterectomy, and it would have been comforting to talk to my mom about all that. Some of our children got married, and we became grandparents, which would have been nice to share with my mom.

If my mom were here, I'd love to ask her many things. There's a health issue going on within our relatives, stemming back to her side of the family. It would be helpful to ask her about how to deal with that. Also, I wish I had paid closer attention to the canning and freezing she did in the kitchen.

It would be interesting to ask her about her experience leaving earth to go to heaven. I wonder what she was thinking and feeling when she waited for her time to come, lying in the hospital bed. She wasn't ambulatory for the whole month of September. Sometimes I sat by her bed and read the Bible to her. I think she heard me.

We have some special memories together of the times when she watched my kids for me. Sometimes, on her birthday or death date, I honor her by posting a photo on social media and saying something about her. I'm in charge of putting flowers on her and my dad's grave in the spring.

I have kept some of my mom's things. I have some bells from her collection. She let me pick some out for my daughters. I have her Bible, some dishes, her cedar chest, and her wedding ring. I have a watch and a necklace she had on in the casket. I enjoyed wearing her wedding dress for my wedding.

There wouldn't be hope if we didn't have Jesus Christ. Without faith, it would be hopeless. You'd live day to day without anything to look forward to. We are promised heaven, and I'm excited to go there. We'll get to be with Jesus and the Father and be with all those who have gone before. We have so many who have gone to heaven already in our family—my mom; Dad; Linda, a special sister-in-law; Joey; Matt, my nephew; and my husband Carl's sister. I look forward to seeing all of them.

Some of my friends are starting to lose their parents now, but many still have their parents. I hope I've helped others when they grieve. A good friend lost her mom years ago, and I tried to be helpful to her.

I'm much more aware now of wanting to be around for my kids. I help out when I can with the grandkids. I'd like my daughters to feel comfortable coming to me if they need something or just to talk. They still like to do things with Mom and Dad at times. Often, they hang out at home, or we all go away together.

The advice I have for women who have lost their mothers is—go to the Lord if you're lonely, read your Bible and pray. Seek out someone to talk with.

When you lose loved ones, it is part of who you are, whether you realize it or not. It's healing to tell my story about my mom.

Bible Verses:

*The LORD is my shepherd, I lack nothing. He makes me lie down in green pastures, he leads me beside quiet waters, he refreshes my soul. He guides me along the right paths for his name's sake. Even though I walk through the darkest valley, I will fear no evil, for you are with me; your rod and your staff, they comfort me. You prepare a table before me in the presence of my enemies. You anoint my head with oil; my cup overflows. Surely your goodness and love will follow me all the days of my life, and I will dwell in the house of the LORD forever. Psalm 23*

## Chapter 30

## I'll Hold Your Right Hand

## With Pat Lubben

*Pat's mom, Alberta, died at age sixty-four, in 1986, when Pat was thirty-nine years old.*

When my mom passed away, I was at her bedside in the hospital, with my whole family. Her death was caused by kidney failure. There wasn't a physical struggle that we could see. She was hooked to many machines and the lines just kept going. All of a sudden, something happened which astounded us. Just seconds before she died, all the numbers on the machines unexpectedly shot way up! Pulse, blood pressure, heart rate, it was all zooming up! All of her systems were engaged or excited. If you looked at her you wouldn't know it, she was just lying there. Things went back down slowly, and then she was gone, which you only knew because the machine's numbers lowered again. If she hadn't been connected to those machines, we wouldn't have seen or known anything was different. We thought that was a precious moment, but I wouldn't venture to guess what it was. Some of my siblings did, but I'm reluctant to speculate. It's a mystery.

Since our family was so large when I was growing up, there wasn't much time to be able to do fun things with my mom. I was the oldest of seven, so I often helped her with work or watched the younger children.

One day, when I was around twelve years old, we had a talk which meant so much to me. I had done something bad. When I went home, I felt very guilty, so I confessed to her what I had done. I was expecting to be in very hot water. I told her I thought I was going to burn in hell. She said she was sure that if I just asked God, He would forgive me. Then she told me a story about something similar she did when she was a child. I felt so loved! I expected her to lower the boom on me and she didn't. She told me I wasn't alone, and all people make mistakes. You can screw up and still be okay. It was an important message!

My mom taught me how to have fun. Before her illness, she was really fun-loving, and my parents were very social and had many friends. She also taught me about commitment because my parents' relationship had peaks and valleys. She especially taught me to be long-suffering. My faith journey was a slow process throughout my childhood because of my mother's wonderful, spiritual influence on me. She loved to go to church, play piano, and sing hymns in our home.

Quite honestly, I feel I didn't really know my mom very well. When I was in high school, she was annoying. Then when I was in college, she was annoying. I came back home briefly, went to Europe for a time, then married, and moved away. She was just Mom, who played her role. I think if she didn't get sick, I would have finally gotten to know her as a real person, adult to adult. As a young person, I was focused on myself. I was concerned with what my career would be, who I would marry, and then I began to have children. Suddenly, the opportunity to get closer to my mother was gone. That's the worst thing. She couldn't tell me her stories or tell me her heart because she suffered a massive stroke. I missed out on knowing her as an adult. I wasn't even interested yet in knowing more than what's on the surface. It's just where you are when you're young.

My mom had a devastating stroke fourteen years before her death, at age fifty, when I was twenty-five years old. She was in a wheelchair from that time until her death. It was very sudden, and she never fully recovered from it. She was in a residential care facility since the age of fifty, as my dad couldn't care for her alone. She had very little use of her hands, her speech was affected, and she had virtually no mobility.

We kind of lost our mom way back at that time. Although we loved her and cared for her, she was never quite the same mom. That was a painful time. I was newly married when it happened. When I had my babies, she couldn't come to help me as other mothers do for their daughters.

We had a few good talks when I was younger, but of course, if I had known, I would have tried to have many more. I was in my early twenties, trying to put my own life together, not concentrating on soaking up as much of my mom as possible. When my first marriage ended in divorce, I really wanted to talk to her about it, but by then she was not able to carry on conversations. She was alive, but very ill. My mom was around until my daughter Natalie was three years old, and my son David was eight. She couldn't be like other grandmothers running around and playing, but they remember her. I missed having her around for the common little everyday things too. In the beginning my dad made sure to get her to family events, but later it was too hard for him as he got older. We visited her, but it's not the same as having her in your home. She communicated some nonverbally, but it wasn't like having a conversation with your mom. I had to invent how to be a mother on my own.

First, she was in a facility in the Chicago area and then several places in Michigan. Eventually, my dad stopped taking her to facilities in hopes of rehabilitation and recovery, to get back to her former self. I visited her often, although I lived in Holland, Michigan, and had small children. She could think clearly and was aware, but it was really hard for her to express herself. I had a serious illness when I was thirty-four, and wished she could have been there for me. It was extremely hard to talk to her on the phone because she spoke very few words over the fourteen years.

My mom's health declined. When she was sixty-four, she was on dialysis for kidney failure in intensive care at the hospital for about ten days. She was not conscious that last day, so we knew the end was probably very close. When my six siblings, my dad, and I were all around her bed that day, they asked me to pray. The sacred moment of her death was upon us.

Following her death, our minister from our church came and talked with us as we discussed some aspects of her funeral. Since it was only a few days before Christmas, he also made a profound and true observation. He talked about how the first Christmas wasn't a fun or happy time; it was dark, lonely, and scary. Christmas is really not about all this "fluff." The funeral attendants came to prepare and take her body. I went home with my dad to his house so he wouldn't be alone that first night.

I spoke at the funeral. I mentioned my parents' fiery relationship. They were either hot or cold. Sometimes, I'd come home from school, and she'd be sitting on his lap. At times, they ran cold, and they'd be angry at each other. They had ups and downs. One of my best memories from my childhood, is when I woke up to music. I crept down the stairs and watched them dancing. That was so cool. They were not passive people.

When I was walking out of the funeral, it was meaningful to see that several of my friends drove a long distance to attend, especially since everyone is so busy just before Christmas.

It helped me to have the whole family together, and experience the blessed numbness you have with death. You really don't feel anything for a while. At least for me, I was on autopilot at first. You just keep doing what needs to be done, and that is somewhat of a gift.

I had some aunts but didn't have much contact with them, as they were spread out around the area and I was such a busy young mom. Now I have two remaining aunts, sisters of my mom. I began to long for deep conversations with them. In the last years, we've gotten close to my Aunt Laura, who lives in Michigan, and we took her to see her sister in Colorado. She's in her nineties, healthy, and living on her own. My mom and Aunt Laura didn't even drive, so her husband would sometimes drop her off at our house in the morning on his way to work, when I was a child. I'd wake up to the sound of the two of them giggling together. I loved the days when she would come over.

As our time together in Colorado was drawing to a close, we were doing a puzzle together, and I asked them, "Would you guys please tell me about my mom?" They looked surprised and said, "Well, she's just like us!" My Aunt Laura is about as close to my mom as you can get; she's very much like her. I always tell her she's my role model. We take her on an excursion every year now. Since her husband died and she doesn't have kids around, she and I developed a closeness. I didn't reach out to her when I was young, but now the opportunity was there. I didn't get to know my own mom adult-to-adult, so this is a special relationship with Aunt Laura. It was wonderful to reconnect with her.

I don't have many possessions from my mom, but I do have her piano. I had earrings, but I gave them to my Aunt Laura because I wasn't wearing them, and she treasures them. Another precious thing is my mom's bathrobe. I forgot all about that until this moment. It's not something I pull out very often but sometimes when I miss her, it's soothing to wrap it around me.

I hope I will do good in the world without knowing it. I hope I touch a lot of people in a caring way, but I don't necessarily want to know I was important in their process. It's not that I don't want the attention, but I don't want that to be the motivation. It boils down to, just be nice, do good in the world. Maybe you did good and will never know it. You never know what helped people and to what extent. So seldom would anyone come back to tell you, you just have to trust you put good stuff out there and hope that has made an impact.

My mom was gone long before most of my friends' parents, so I understand and care when I see someone go through the death of someone close. I'm not sure I help them, but maybe I do without knowing it. I think her death made me feel like I was on my own. It brought it home in a very vivid way, that bad things happen and it's unavoidable.

If you have lost your mother, I'm sorry. I feel like I should have something really wise or profound to say, but I don't. It's sad. It's terrible. It always hurts. It scabs over a bit, but it's one of those losses you just don't get over. It helps to talk with others about your mom. I have a group of friends who've met for years around Mother's Day, and we share something about our mothers, which is a precious time.

It was a surprise that it still hurts when I talk about my mother. I don't talk about it anymore, and it was so long ago. My siblings are the only other ones who knew my mom. We went through the same experience. Every once in a while, my younger single brother, who lives where we grew up with my parents, will email me. He'll say something like "I was mowing the lawn and came across Mom's favorite perennial." He'll send a picture of it. It's nice that he experienced the same mom and talks about it occasionally.

I appreciate my life now. God is good. I'm enjoying this stage of life and it's pleasant. My family, friends, and work are good. God has been with me all along and will continue to be my rock.

Bible Verse:

*For I, the LORD your God, hold your right hand; it is I who say to you, "Fear not, I am the one who helps you."* Isaiah 41:13 ESV

I love that image of God taking ahold of my right hand. I cling to this verse or send it to my children when they need a verse.

# Chapter 31

## The Peace of Knowing

## With Julie Peters

*Julie's age at the time of the interview was forty-three. Her mom, Sharon, died at the age of sixty-two, on March 19, 2010, when Julie was thirty-seven.*

My cousin, Lori, was at their home when my mom was in the process of dying, and called my dad in. I was okay with not being there for her last moment of life because I treated every day like it might be her last. When I got back, she was still warm. I've never hated cancer as much as while watching her those last few weeks of her life. She had been lying there for sixteen days without moving. When I saw her bed empty, I cried. That's when it hit me.

Originally, we found out my mom had cancer, in 1989 when I was a senior in high school. The first time, she had breast cancer, had a mastectomy, did some treatments and went into remission. We thought she was done with it.

My parents were such a great example in their marriage and in life. I saw my mom's servant heart daily. Every morning, she had her Bible open in the living room. It was all marked up, with papers stuck in it. As a late teen and young adult, I kept trying to give it all to God, focusing on finding joy in the reoccurrence of cancer. Faith in God carried us through the ups and downs.

She prayed for all of her kids' spouses every day since we were born. Sometimes when I forget to pray for my kids, I think my mom surely would be praying for them. I believe she was close to Jesus every day, and I also strive for that kind of closeness to Him.

Later we found out the cancer was in her chest wall, intestines, and finally in her liver. Trenton, my oldest, was only a baby when I went to the hospital to see her. She was healthy for a while, and it would come back. She even did some alternative treatments. I struggled a great deal when she first got liver cancer. I was in an *Experiencing God* Bible study, and the light came on in my mind that I needed to let her go and trust God. She was His daughter long before she was my mom. Every day I had her was a blessing. Even when she was first diagnosed, when I was in high school, I had done some of my grieving. It was a long process. Not that I didn't struggle at times. I sure did.

Even during many years of being in horrible pain, she was coordinating *Helping Hands*, a program at our church that supplies meals to those in need. She served my dad as he worked massive hours on the farm, and she participated in several ministries at church. My mom focused on others, which kept her from having a pity party. She showed such a servant heart during her life.

Almost every year, my mom took my two sisters-in-law and me, on a shopping trip for a weekend in the fall. Some years she didn't feel very well but got through it. We'd buy outfits for the kids, go out to lunch, and had a great time. She helped me get groceries when my oldest three were young. They were all so close in age, so it was helpful. She had a cart, and I had a double cart. My children and I spent a great amount of time with my mom in the last four years of her life. We made many simple memories going out or being together on the farm. Most of my kids remember quite a bit about spending time with their grandma. After she passed away, I was very thankful for those times.

As my kids were growing, I wanted to set a good example for them. We had many talks with our six kids because we knew my mom's death would probably occur. We told them, "It's okay to grieve or cry. God has a plan, and He knows best." I didn't hide my sadness, and let them see me cry at times. We talked openly about my mom and her illness.

My parents spent winters in Arizona, and my mom really wanted to go that last time, although she was quite sick. The day before they were going to leave, they were watching my kids, and when we came to pick them up and were talking, she had a seizure. It was determined to be a brain tumor; cancer had moved into her brain. They still left for Arizona. My mom really loved it there. She dealt with cancer and bad side effects for twenty years. They did radiation in Arizona, but her health continued to go downhill. She was in extreme pain because a blockage was squeezing her intestines and no food could get through. She had many ups and downs through the years, but she was declining.

My husband and I went on a vacation to Mexico during that time. I talked to her on the phone every day. Those last conversations were a huge blessing. She was feeling guilty for wanting to be done. I spoke of giving her permission to go. She wanted to make sure I knew how much she loved me. She was selfless and didn't want to burden anyone.

I had a close relationship with my mom. Although there didn't seem to be anything wrong between us, I still made sure to apologize in case there was something I had done that I might not have even known about. I wasn't a wild teenager but did the normal things teenagers and young adults do.

They flew back from Arizona on March 1. My brothers and I went to the airport to pick them up. She had lost all her hair, and her skin was so gray that I didn't recognize her. I don't know how she endured the flight, she was so weak, but we tried not to show our shock. In my mind, I questioned if she'd make the car ride home. She came home because she wanted to see all her kids and grandkids one more time. She stayed at their home on the farm. We called hospice as soon as they came home, and they had someone come at least once a day to help out. It was hard for some of the grandkids to see her. They went in to talk to her and kept it very short. My youngest was only two years old.

My mom could only talk or mumble the first few days, then was unresponsive for her final days. We cared for her, and took turns staying through the night so my dad could sleep. We didn't give her water anymore because she couldn't eat or swallow. I was struggling with guilt and felt like we were killing her. One of the hospice nurses, Ann, was so awesome and talked me through it. She said, "The cancer is doing it." She was such a gentle, soft-spoken spirit. I knew we were doing the right thing, but it was so hard.

I was there every day even when it wasn't my turn to stay overnight because I lived only two miles down the country road. On the night she passed, I went home at ten o'clock at night. My cousin, Lori, who is a nurse, planned to stay overnight. I barely made it home before my dad called. Honestly, we had been praying for days that God would take her or heal her, one or the other. Of course, I was still praying for a miracle to the end, but she wouldn't have wanted to live in her condition.

At the funeral visitation, all the grandkids wrote her a note to put in the casket with her. Our kids leaned over and kissed her on the forehead. She had a wig, as she had lost all her hair. It sounds terrible, but she looked better in her casket than she had in the last weeks at home because of all the makeup. At the visitations, I didn't cry much.

One comment from a friend, Pam, at the visitation, has stuck with me. Her mom passed away, and she told me to make sure you keep your family together. She commented that your mom has probably been the one who made sure you gather at the holidays and other occasions. I, being the oldest and the only girl, would be the one to carry on that tradition. I thought that was great advice and have tried to do that.

My mom had picked out a song she wanted at her funeral. She picked, "How Great Thou Art." I couldn't listen to that song for years without crying. I also wanted, "Blessed Be the Name of the Lord." My brother Ryan gave a touching tribute.

In her last weeks at home, and at the funeral and cemetery, I even took photographs. It sounds crazy, but I did it in case I wanted them later. I didn't want to regret not having them and wanted to keep her memory alive. A lot of the grandkids struggled when she was lowered into the ground. That seems so final.

You have to mourn and go through the process and then move on. You can't stay in one place. We told our kids how much Grandma would love to be here for special occasions like my oldest son, Trenton's graduation from high school.

Because we discussed my mom openly over the years, the oldest ones still mention her occasionally. My oldest daughter went to a week-long camp about grief. They draw pictures of their loved one, write about and talk about them. We had a lot of communication and good conversations at home over the years. My oldest ones have happy memories of doing things with my mom. They say, "Remember when Grandma baked, she would let us eat the cookie dough?" Or, "She would shake us upside-down to get the grumpy bugs out of us when we were crabby."

I have a wonderful mother-in-law, but they live far away out in South Dakota. Even this week, I was painting and thought how nice it would be to show my mom. It's just the little stuff like that. Or your kid does something you're proud of, and you want to tell your mom because she would be so excited. Those kid moments your mom would love to hear. Potty training victories, when they got their first deer, first big fish, awesome school grades, or ACT scores, that's the stuff we'd talk about.

On the special dates, I usually call my dad to see how he's doing. A neat thing about her death date is that my niece, Josie Sharon, was born on the same day, two years later and was named after her. We said God reclaimed the day for good.

My dad keeps most of her belongings for now, but we got to pick out a few things. We also let the granddaughters pick out something special. Mother's Day is the hardest for me, which shocked me at first. I thought it would be Christmas because it was my mom's favorite holiday. She would buy way too many gifts. Some days, I'm just kind of in a funk. I'm not crying the whole day or anything but just not my normal self. The oddest things might make you cry. I would have thought one thing would set me off, and then it was this other random thing instead.

You might never know if you've influenced someone or made a difference with them, but I talk to a gal I work with, that lost her mom. I ask her how she's doing, give her a hug, or she talks. I try to listen.

Sometimes people aren't sure if they should approach me about my mom. At times, a person would talk to me, I'd cry, and they'd say they were sorry. I'd tell them it was okay that I was crying. They were genuinely interested and trying to help. You want people to ask and remember your loved one. It's nice that they care how you're doing. I don't feel bad if someone cries when I talk to them about their loved one who has passed away. I don't say much when I go to funeral visitations or funerals. I say, "I'm sorry for your loss," or "I'm praying for you." The normal cliché stuff. Just being there is what matters.

Your life will never be the same when you lose your mother, but it can still be good if you can focus on the memories and the positive things and don't let bitterness and anger grow. You need to mourn and miss her, but keep praying for peace. That's the one thing I got those years before, the peace of knowing God loves her more than I love her. You need to grieve and cry, but don't stay there. Sometimes when we go through tough things, God grows us. We do what we can here, focusing on the positive, but it's a temporary world.

My son, Brennan, just asked me in the car today, "Mom, do you ever still cry about Grandma?" I said, "No, not too often. But I always will miss her on this earth. I know I will see her again in heaven."

It's good to talk about my mom again. Sometimes I get so caught up in the busyness of life and family, I don't take the time to savor the memories.

Bible Verses:

*Trust in the LORD with all your heart, and lean not on your own understanding.* Proverbs 3:5 NKJV

This is my favorite verse. Trust. If you can trust Him, and have peace in that, then the rest just falls into place.

# Chapter 32

## It's Time for Me to Go

## With Jodi Vande Noord

*Jodi's mom, Sandi, died in 2006, at the age of fifty-five, when Jodi was thirty-one. She was forty-one years old at the time of the interview.*

When I was nineteen years old, I was about to begin my sophomore year at Calvin College, in Grand Rapids, Michigan. A few days before I had to leave from our Pella, Iowa, home, my mom was diagnosed with breast cancer at the age of forty-four. When I left, they didn't know how severe it was or which treatment plan they would utilize. Getting in the car and heading off to college was very difficult for me. She had a mastectomy to remove one breast. Then she did chemotherapy and radiation. After all that was done, she was cancer-free for six years.

Since I was the only girl, my mom and I went on shopping trips to Des Moines when I was in grade school, high school, college, and when I was married. We'd go to Kohl's or the mall, or out to eat. That was our special thing to do together. My mom prepared me for difficulties in life. She told me life isn't all fun and games. Sometimes, you have to be more serious or responsible. Everyone's different and they don't beat the same drum. We have to be tolerant of that. In a way, God might have been preparing me for losing her.

I had a strong faith in God, and so did my mom. I was raised with faith because my parents were strong Christians. When I was out on my own, I finally took my faith more seriously. Part of me thought I didn't need the faith my parents had. This was long before my mom died, but some difficult circumstances made me realize life can be hard. I needed the Lord. I was in my early twenties when I began to learn things can't always go my way. I think I was spoiled by having everything done for me.

I got married and had both of my kids during the years she was in remission. It never occurred to us cancer would return. We all thought she was past it. She felt good, was putting weight back on, and doing her normal activities for six years. There were some really good years during that time.

When my husband and I went on vacation to Canada, I was reading the sequel to *The Prayer of Jabez*, called, *Secrets of the Vine*, by Bruce Wilkerson. It was just before my mom got diagnosed the second time, and she had come to our house to stay with our one-year-old son. I was outside in the beautiful nature and thinking I wanted to center my life around God and figure out His will for my life. This was a time of spiritual growth for me, which I would need in the coming days and years.

She thought she had beat cancer and lived normally until 2001. Because of back pain, she thought she had a slipped disk, but an MRI revealed fourteen tumors in her spine. Cancer had returned. She went through treatments again for about four years, but it just kept spreading to her lungs, liver, and stomach. She tried anything the doctors suggested, such as injections, chemo pills, or radiation pills, but nothing worked this time.

Two years before she died, there was a time when I realized she wasn't going to make it. The cancer was going to beat her. She was slowly failing. It was a hard thing to accept.

My kids kept me going through those hard times because they were small and required a lot of my attention. It was a good distraction. I had my purpose in them, taking care of their needs, preschool, and everything that comes with little kids. I was not myself for a long time, but I focused on being a good parent.

There were so many signs of my mom's faith. Even toward the end, many circumstances allowed me to see how strong her faith was. While she was sick, she told me she constantly prayed for a cure and treatments.

She would get emotional every year at Easter. It was her favorite time because she was so humbled by what Jesus did for her. A movie called, *The Passion of the Christ,* came out, including a very graphic portrayal of the death of Jesus. She could never go to the movie because she had a hard-enough time thinking about it.

When she went through cancer the second time, every time she went to the doctor, she asked what treatment they could try next. She was determined to beat it because she wanted to be around for her grandkids. My son was five years old, and my daughter was one when she passed away. A few weeks before she died, a home health nurse finally had to tell her, "Sandi, there are no more treatments, nothing else to try, this is it. This is going to be the end."

Mom said, "Okay." She was coherent even though she had a tumor in her brain. She got quieter after that, and it was hard to get her to talk. She no longer walked. She decided to die at home, so hospice came in. Once she laid down, I think she decided that was it, and it was her time to go.

We gathered around her and waited. Her breath began to be very labored. She took deep breaths, almost gasping. She breathed deeply for about fifteen breaths, and then she just stopped breathing. My Dad, his mom, me, and my brother and his wife, were all in the living room together when she passed away. My personality is such that I don't want to miss anything, so I watched while the funeral home attendants undressed her and put her into a zippered bag.

Many family members had to come from other states, so we waited a few days to have the funeral visitation and funeral. When we pulled up to the church for the visitation, it was heart-wrenching for me when I saw the hearse. She had requested an open casket, and we had pictures of her life playing in a slide show. During that time, I didn't get emotional because I was so busy and distracted by all the people. I think it was busy because she was a bit of a younger person, and lots of my friends came too, some from a great distance. It went way beyond the designated time. I'm not usually much of a crier, but the second day when we were saying our final good-byes, and they closed the casket for the last time, I realized how final it was.

It was a freezing cold March day in Iowa. To top it off, an unusual snowstorm blew in, which annoyed me. According to one of my neighbors, the deceased person's favorite weather happens on their funeral day. That was true of my mom—she really loved the snow. My dad requested to do her burial first at the cemetery, with immediate family. It was very cold and snowy. I sat under a tent. The pastor spoke some words. We took some flowers from the top of her casket. I stayed longer than anyone else and watched them lower her casket into the ground. I thought, *Don't put her in the ground, that's my mom!*

Next came the funeral. It was held in my parents' church, where I was baptized and married. My family met in a back room before it started, so we were all together. I felt somewhat of a relief there because the hardest part for me was the burial. During the funeral, I began thinking, *Okay, we're going to live through this.*

The pastor shared a memory on my behalf. I had a dream about a month before my mom died. She and I were walking along. She had a kerchief on her head because of the cancer treatments. She said to me, "It's time for me to go." I tried to keep her there; I even grabbed her arms. I said, "No! Don't go!" She pulled her arms away and said, "I have to go. You're going to be fine." Then she disappeared. I haven't thought about that in a very long time. It gave me comfort later. I'm thankful God gave me that dream.

At the end of the service, the organist and pianist played "The Hallelujah Chorus" together. That's what my mom wanted to have, as she was very musical. After the funeral, I felt release that the hardest parts were over.

After my mom died, I was so much more aware of my mom as I mothered my kids. Especially the first year after she died, when I'd say something to my kids, I felt like it was my mom talking. I said things like, "If you can't say something nice, don't say anything at all!" When that happened, it made me sad, but at the same time I would smile. It was that weird in-between stage when you're smiling because of the memory, but you're sad she's gone.

My kids didn't know any different and have always considered my dad's wife their grandma after he remarried, and she's a wonderful grandma to my kids. They didn't know my mom because they were so young when she died. But I want to keep my mom's memories alive, so I make sure to talk about their Grandma Sandi.

I still had both of my grandmas. Even though they lived out of state, they were both very kind to me, and I talked to them on the phone quite often. They were comforting and helpful. Faith, who was a good friend of my mom's, is now a special friend to me. Once a year, she still has me over for breakfast to chat. In the beginning, we talked about my mom more, but now we usually catch up on life.

Since my mom has been gone, I wished she could have seen things, like my son's eighth-grade graduation or my daughter in the Christmas program. I wish we had been able to talk more about death while she was alive. My mom couldn't admit she was going to die, and it was a taboo subject. I wish we could have just hashed it out and talked about how I would see her again someday and that we'd all survive the separation. We could have reminisced about her fun memories of her life. We never said those words out loud because it was so heartbreaking. Now, I'd like to talk to her about what heaven is like, who she sees there, and who she spends time with. I'm curious if she can see what's going on here on earth.

In the first few years after her death, my dad, brother, and I talked about her before opening our Christmas gifts, but we don't do that anymore. Christmas was such a big deal to her. I go to the cemetery sometimes to remember her. If we're together for a birthday, someone might mention something they remember about my mom. My husband, and my brother's wife both knew her. I have her picture on my mantelpiece. I have some of her jewelry, bags, and purses. I know it sounds weird, but I kept one of her deodorant containers after I cleaned out her bathroom. I kept it for years just to set it out in my bathroom to remember her. I have some of her scarves and gloves. I have her Bible, which she wrote in, and it's special to see her handwriting.

Dying doesn't scare me like it used to. My experience with death makes me feel so much closer to the Lord. He gives me hope and comfort from the Holy Spirit and the promise of heaven. To this day, if someone is under hospice care, I find myself sometimes wanting to be there. That's where I feel God the most, with someone who's almost with God in heaven. Not that I'm in a hurry to die but happy that heaven awaits us.

Soon after my mom died, I wrote down memories from the last few weeks of her life. I printed out a book of about sixty pages to give to people who have lost a parent or grandparent. I gave copies to my friends and relatives, and there's also a copy in the hospice house of Pella, for visitors to read. It tells my mom's experience and how I saw the Lord working through the whole process. I keep copies around and give it out when I think people could benefit from it.

Everybody handles death differently, and no one should feel guilty about how they handle it. They have to do what's right for them. When I was young, I thought I had to do or feel things a certain way. There's no right or wrong. It just depends on the person and their relationship with their mother.

Talking about my mom's story made me discover, I still had some tears around! I feel glad that she could help others through what she and I experienced. I think my mom would smile about me telling her story.

Bible Verses:

*But we do not want you to be uninformed, brothers, about those who are asleep, that you may not grieve as others do who have no hope.* 1 Thessalonians 4:13 ESV

I had not heard this verse or paid attention to it before my mom's death. Someone wrote this verse in a sympathy card to me. It helped me a lot through the grieving process, to know we do have hope. This isn't the end for us.

*My heart was grieved and my spirit embittered, yet I am always with you; you hold me by my right hand. You guide me with your counsel, and afterward you will take me into glory.* Psalm 73:21,23–24

One of my mom's favorites:

*For the LORD is good and his love endures forever; his faithfulness continues through all generations.* Psalm 100:5

This was so applicable to her death, because there were four generations in our family when she died. She left her parents, her children, and her grandchildren, and she was the one who had to go first.

# IN THEIR FIFTIES WHEN MOM DIED

# Chapter 33

## Be Available

## With Prudy Berghorst

*Prudy was sixty-eight at the time of the interview. She was fifty years old in 1997, when her mom, Hazel, passed away at the age of seventy-eight years old.*

My dad called to tell me my mom was in the hospital. She was diagnosed with pneumonia, but the doctor put her on antibiotics and said she would be fine in a couple days, so I figured she was going to improve quickly.

The next day I called the hospital. The nurse asked, "Have you talked to your dad?"

She had the head nurse get on the phone and tell me, "I'm so sorry, your mom just died."

It was all very sudden. I was in shock. A friend told me later that I just groaned. She had been healthy and active, and I didn't expect her to die. This was before cell phones. I tried to call my dad first but couldn't get him. He hadn't had the heart to call us yet.

After I called my siblings, we met at my sister Patty's house, all very shaken. We couldn't reach our dad for about an hour. He was driving around and ended up at a friend's house. He was at her side when she died. She had taken a turn for the worst; they had taken an X-ray, got her on oxygen, and she suddenly passed away. He said there was a helpless look on her face, and there was nothing he could do.

It was a shocking way to find out our mom died. I hadn't seen them in six months because they lived in Florida, and all of us kids lived in

Michigan. It turned out that she had congestive heart failure, and it was more serious than they thought. She drowned in her own secretions. We don't know exactly what happened, and for a while, we toyed with the idea to have it more closely investigated, but that wouldn't bring her back.

My parents had a loving, God-filled, fifty-year marriage. My dad was overcome with shock and grief and didn't know what to do. I thought about flying down there. My dad considered having her cremated, but all of us kids said we needed to see her face. He came home with her on a plane. One of the saddest moments of my life is when my dad, who was such a big-chested, robust man, got off the plane looking so broken. My two sisters and I surrounded him and cried. We were devastated for my dad and for us.

My mom's body was prepared in Florida, so we had to wait a couple days to get everything organized with the funeral home in Holland, Michigan. Crowds of people came to the visitations. All the grandchildren came too. My parents had lived in several places and had a grocery business. They were very well known. We had the funeral at Central [Church], where most of my family attended. We wanted people to know what she was like. Our dad was more boisterous, and mom was quieter. Much of our family is very talkative like our dad, so the pastor joked that he didn't know if she ever had time to get a word in edgewise. The funeral was hard. I cried a lot.

I had a birthday a week before she died. My parents had sent me a pink Bible, so I called to thank them. My dad was usually the one to answer and talk, but this time, by God's design, I had a chance to talk to my mom for about thirty minutes. It was so nice to have that last conversation with my mom on Thursday, and she died on Monday. Later it plagued me whether I remembered to say, "I love you" or not.

My mom had beautiful white hair. At the funeral, she looked wonderful because she hadn't been ill and because of embalming, she didn't have any wrinkles. She didn't like her wrinkles as she got older, so we said she would be proud. She wore her red dress and pearls. I appreciated that she looked so nice the last time I got to see her. I have those pearls today.

My mom was a writer and wrote stories for the Sunday school paper and was able to have some published. My dad later married Bunnie. Out of kindness to her, we haven't sorted through a lot of my mom's writings. My dad has now passed away too, and we're giving her space. It will be neat to see my mom's many stories, with her own handwriting, on paper.

My mom never told us that she was raised in a conflicted home, where she was sexually abused. My dad told us after she died. When my grandpa died, I wondered why she didn't shed a tear. Then I knew why. Back then, nothing was done about that kind of thing. My dad and mom knew each other since childhood, and he rescued her from that situation and also brought her to the Lord in their teens. If you couldn't find my mom, she was reading her Bible or praying over us kids. She was a wonderful testimony to me throughout my life, with a quiet demeanor and strong faith. I was raised in a home where the first thing I heard in the morning, and the last thing I heard at night, was them praying together. From my bedroom, before I got up, I heard them praying at the breakfast table. When I was twelve years old, we went to an evangelist. When I wanted to take Jesus into my heart, my parents prayed with me, which seemed a natural thing to do, because of our faith-filled home growing up.

My mom was a very positive person. When I was a young teenager, I always felt I had awful hair, and she said to me, "Oh honey, it looks so clean and shiny." She wasn't a hugger. I understand that now. I rested my head on my mom's shoulder in church and she'd stroke my hair. She wasn't a demonstrative person, but those little touches made me feel very loved.

As a young adult, when leaving my parents' home, my mom, the *Scrabble* barracuda, often asked, "Why don't you stay and play *Scrabble*?"

Usually, I'd say I had to get going even when I could have stayed. I regret not spending more time with my mom. When I was middle-aged, I'm thankful that my fifteen-year old daughter and I lived with my parents for a couple years while I was finishing grad school, as a single mom, after my husband died. I was going through a very rough time, and we have good memories of that precious time that really helped me out. My mom was such a great cook, and the deal was that she would cook dinner and I would clean it up.

After mom died, we knew she was in heaven. We were confident that she was happy. It was a different kind of grief as time went on. Sometimes grief washes over you. You'll be fine, then something will hit you and make you cry. My grandparents had died. My mom's side of the family were not Christians, and we hardly ever saw them. My dad's relations were scattered all over the US. My twin sister and I became even closer.

On her birthday each year, I think about her. It makes me feel closer to her when I touch her pearls and wear them to church. When I use her china, I say out loud, "This is for you, Mom." My mom didn't use it much although they drank a lot of tea. She saved it for very special occasions. I use it often, and have added onto the set of *Old Country Rose* or the teapots. I also have a teddy bear someone made for each us out of my mom's fur coat.

I'd love to tell my mom some special things. She was concerned about my youngest child. Now she could see that she's married to a wonderful man, has children, and a successful career. My other children were out of the house when my husband and mom died, and my "in the house" mothering was done. They died only seven years apart, so the grief becomes intermingled. I talk to my children almost every day and make sure to say, "I love you." You never know when it's going to be the last time, so it's important not to leave anything unsaid. My mom and my current husband, John, would enjoy getting to know one another. I didn't expect to get married again, but after twelve years, the Lord had a different plan. My mom would be so happy for me to have a man like him.

My mom taught me a great deal. She was a pray-er. She taught me the value of reading the Word and praying, by her example. I've learned to take prayer seriously. If I say I will pray for someone, I write it down and do it. A vision always sticks in my mind of my mom kneeling by her bed, red Bible in her hands. We knew not to bother her. It was a beautiful thing to have, but you don't appreciate that kind of thing as much until you get older. She surely was a woman of God.

When I was a nurse, and patients were really sick, often the family asked me, "Do you think I should stay?" I would say, "If you would feel bad if you didn't stay, then you should stay." I also told them that their loved one could probably hear them, and you should say what you need to, even if you think they can't hear you.

As believers, I know we will all be together again in heaven, which is a great comfort. We don't know what heaven is like, but I know my mom is waiting. We don't sorrow the same way others sorrow. I personally do not know how people walk through losses without Christ in their lives.

The death of my mom taught me to offer the gift of time to my brothers, sisters, dad, kids, and grandkids. My mom was available. She was a quiet person but did a very good job of being there when I needed it. I strive to do that for others, and often make myself as accessible as possible to my kids or grandkids.

If someone has lost their mother, I say, focus on positive things about your mom and try to incorporate those into your own life. If you have some forgiving to do, do it! If she wasn't all she should have been as a mom, she was probably doing the best she could. Forgive, and let go of the bad things. You can forgive them even after they're gone. You only hurt yourself if you hang onto unforgiveness. For my own mom, there wasn't anything to forgive her for. When we were all together, she would be quiet, just listening and enjoying her family. She was a deep thinker who took great joy and pride in her children. I often voice my feelings and memories about her and show her pictures to my children and grandchildren so that she lives on in their memories. Not many of them got to know her and I want them to know what she was like.

It was so good to talk about my mom again and bring her to mind. I forgot what a prayer warrior she was, and she always had a pleasant word about everyone. She never said bad things about people and was not a gossip. Sometimes I forget how much I miss her.

I'm grateful I had my mom around until she was seventy-eight. I'm reminded to cherish each day, because you never know what life is going to bring.

Bible Verse:

*As a mother comforts her child, so will I comfort you.* Isaiah 66:13

I hung onto that. God comforts me!

## Chapter 34

## This is the Day that the Lord Has Made

## With Marcia

*Marcia was sixty-five years old at the time of the interview. Her mom, Hermina, was eighty-four when she died, December 18, 2006, when Marcia was fifty-four years old.*

After spending most of the day with my mom at the hospice house, I went home to have supper with my husband. Although the roads were really bad that December day, I told my husband, "I just have to go back. Something tells me I need to go back." My mom had been failing in the last few days. When I arrived in her room, she was having bad Cheyne-Stokes breathing. That's when they have very loud, uneven breathing. I called a nurse in, and she agreed I should call my family, although she said it could be a short or a long time. My brother was planning to come that evening, but she died before he, or anyone else could get there.

My mom's faith was evident because she lived it every day. She'd do anything for anyone, and you could tell she had a vibrant prayer life. As I was growing up, it was normal to see her kneeling by the bed praying or reading her Bible. She talked openly about her faith. She taught us all about Christ and wanted us to know Him. Mom was the driving force in our spiritual upbringing and a stabilizing factor in our home. She sent us to Sunday school, catechism, and other Christian activities.

My mom was very well-liked in the community, and she was the oldest of ten. My mom's youngest siblings said she was like a mom to them. My grandmother, her mom, had lung and breast cancer, so my mom quit school after sixth grade to take care of her mom and siblings. She later cared for her mom at our home when I was growing up. My grandma died when I was in junior high school. My mom was a very service-oriented person and was a caretaker most of her life. We did life together as I helped her with daily chores and activities. She also took over the driving for her mother-in-law, volunteered in church, and helped my aunt who lived next door. My mom had some very big losses in her life. She lost a daughter, a granddaughter, and later my dad passed away.

I was brought up in a Christian home and have believed all my life. When I was a teenager, I attended a class at church and made a public profession of faith, at the age when you're expected to do it. The thing that really made me think seriously was when my older sister, Marilyn, was killed in an automobile accident. I thought, *What if it had been me?* I embraced the faith much more after that.

My mom had a series of health issues. She had diabetes and heart failure, but the main thing at the end was kidney failure. She was off and on dialysis, moving between her home and my home. After a broken pelvis from a car accident, we tried to take care of her at home, but she finally said it was too hard on us kids. She said we had busy families, and it was best for her to go. We couldn't regulate her medications well enough, and she had pain. She was very accommodating and never wanted to put anyone out. Toward the end, it was her idea to go to Sheldon Meadows, an assisted living facility.

Later, they remembered her at Sheldon Meadows, and said my mom was a joy. She got up every morning and said, "This is the day that the Lord has made, let us rejoice and be glad in it." She portrayed that to everyone around her until the end. She went to Butterworth Hospital with heart problems; the heart catheterization used a dye which gave her allergic complications. She needed dialysis, and it was too hard to bring her back and forth for catheterization too. At that time, she made the decision on her own not to continue the dialysis, saying it was too hard on everyone else to drive her three times a week.

The closeness of family, and knowing my mom had a strong faith in God, helped me through. She lived a good life, and said she was ready to go. In fact, one day her minister came to the hospice house when I was there. She asked him to pray that she would die quickly. At the time, I thought, *Oh no.* It hit me hard, but yet it was a comfort too.

When my mom was in the hospice house, she wasn't responsive the last couple of days. I read to her, talked to her a bit, and held her hand. I think she knew I was there. Whether it was my wish or that she really knew, I'm not sure. I said, "It's okay, Mom, I'm here." It was especially hard to listen to that low, guttural breathing. Being the only one there when she died was special but also very difficult. I was really glad I went back, and I would have been devastated if I hadn't. After the calls to my brother and sister, I called my husband Rog. That's when I cried hard.

We all met to discuss the funeral plans and arrangements. Each of our spouses came along as well and it wasn't too stressful. My brother is a very steady person and was a huge help. He took over my late dad's business and knew the finances. I appreciated everything he did during that time.

At the funeral, we sang, "Great Is thy Faithfulness," which has extra meaning now. I woke up to that song after I had an emergency liver procedure done in Tennessee. I believe the Holy Spirit put it in my mind. Hearing it again at my mom's funeral was touching.

After my mom's death, we had to divide up my parents' possessions. We hadn't dispersed any items after my dad's death, so now we were forced to do it. We went through everything and asked, "Do you want it?" If one person wanted it, they got it. If more than one person wanted it, we put their names into a hat and drew one name, to avoid any hard feelings. If it was a bigger item, the person even paid money for it. The two-day process was demanding, but I thought it was fair and worked well. I'm thankful we got it over with, without fighting over stuff. They're only material possessions.

My kids were already graduated from college when she died, so they did have her for a good portion of their lives. I think the whole thing affected the kind of grandmother I am. I do more with my grandchildren. I fully love to babysit the grandkids when I can, and wouldn't want them to pay for a babysitter. It feels like I'm getting paid when I get to take care of them, and I feel very blessed.

Both of my kids missed my mom because they spent a lot of time together. She was at our house almost every Sunday for dinner. She met both of my kids' future partners but didn't live until their weddings. Both of them put a candle out at their ceremonies, in honor of their grandma. My daughter had a slide show at her wedding about passing down the legacy of faith. Both of their weddings were hard for me because they were relatively soon after my mom's death. One of them also played, "Great Is thy Faithfulness," and of course, I teared up just before I had to walk down the aisle. Mom would have really loved to be at their weddings.

There was a time when I called someone when I wished I could call my mom. My daughter wanted to make Grandma's pickles. But my mom put seven different pickle recipes in the church recipe book, so we didn't know which one we should make. I called her friend, Jo, because she was someone about my mom's age who knew her. She knew which recipe it was. In fact, she even gave my daughter a crock to put them in, which was specifically for fermenting pickles.

A lot of things come up that make me want to ask her opinion. Little things, like, where's that recipe, or about my children or family. In some ways, it seems longer than nine years ago, and sometimes it seems like yesterday. There are many times I think I would just like to call my mom, and then I remember I can't. I'd love to ask her what heaven is like. Since I lost my mom later than a lot of people, I had plenty of opportunities to ask her things, so I'm thankful.

At the holidays, we make her special cranberry salad. I always remember that September 20 was her birthday, and December 18 was her death date. Of course, that first Christmas was hard without her. We opened gifts from my mom, because she had my sister-in-law purchase them early.

People enjoy my cooking, and I know I acquired that skill from my mom. When I was young, my mom did a lot of cooking and baking, and we were homebodies. After I was married, she came to my house whenever I needed help with anything, such as canning, or just to talk. I can't peel peaches as fast as she could. She wore the skin off her finger and had to wear a bandage. Five of us—my daughter, my daughter-in-law, me, my youngest sister-in-law, and her daughter—get together to carry on my mom's tradition of making chocolate covered cherries every year before Christmas.

She taught me many physical things, but I absorbed much of her quiet and steady nature by being around her. I don't get excited about things very quickly, and can stay calm and organized under pressure. I think it's somewhat genetic. Those kind of things are caught and not taught.

I got to keep some special things from my mom. I got the grandfather clock, teacups, and saucers, and of course, I have all her old recipes. My daughter has something very special from her grandma. When she was a teenager, my mom gave her a book that she wrote answers in. An example of a question is, "What's the worst thing that happened to you in grade school?" The grandma fills out the book of memories to give to her granddaughter.

I've been a mentor for my sister-in-law. You just feel for them when they lose their moms. They need an advocate to tell them, "You might want to call your mom. You aren't crazy. You will make it." I empathize with those who have lost their mothers, especially if they're young. I think I'm more solemn now when I think of my mom. I did appreciate her, but so much more so now. We did a lot together, but you always wish for more time, no matter how old they are when they die.

All I can say to those who have lost their mothers— it's hard. There's just no replacement. Losing a father or sister is hard, but totally different. I pray for those who've lost their moms, differently than I pray for other people— with my heart more than with my mind. When I go to a funeral visitation, lots of times I don't say anything, but just give them a hug. Words don't always help, and sometimes words you may think are comforting may not be. Since I don't know their whole story, I might say the wrong thing, so I try to be quiet.

My greatest desire is that all of my children and grandchildren will have Jesus Christ in their hearts like I do. That's the only thing that gives true hope. Anything else isn't solid at all.

It's always good to remember my mom. I was privileged to have a great childhood with many fond memories.

Bible Verse:

*Now to him who is able to do immeasurably more than all we ask or imagine, according to his power that is at work within us.* Ephesians 3:20

God has always been with me when I went through hard times.

# Chapter 35

## Deeper Than a Best Friend

## With Hope Doolaard

*Hope was fifty-one at the time of the interview.*
*Hope's mom, Arlene, died at age eighty-one, on May*
*12, 2014, when Hope was fifty years old.*

From December to April, my mother visited doctors all over West Michigan. After watching my brother die from pancreatic cancer, she was totally convinced she had it too, even though all the biopsies and tests said she didn't have it. She began to suffer despite a heavy pharmaceutical pain regimen. Physically, she began to struggle and lost weight quickly. The medications didn't control her pain, but the specialists kept saying she didn't have the disease.

I tried to encourage her, with comments like, "They're saying it's not pancreatic cancer." But that disease is pretty hard to ignore, and I'd seen it before. The possibility scared me. My dad and brother had been so sick, thin, and couldn't eat. In some sense, I think people know their own bodies pretty well. Especially women. If they admit it.

My world became consumed with her care, and I just about lived at her house. She was feeling so sick, and we didn't know why. Thank the Lord, I was able to juggle things around to be there with her. I had a family life, a job, and my kids were both still living at home. We said, "Praise the Lord it's not cancer." She kept saying, "They're missing something."

She didn't want to go to Mayo, but she had so much pain and no answers. I bought plane tickets to Mayo without telling her. I sat next to her, grabbed her hand, and asked her, "Mom, what would you say if I had tickets to Mayo? Would you go?"

With a slight glimmer of hope in her eyes, with her weak voice, she uttered, "Yes."

"Well, that's good, because you're going tomorrow." I said. She and my sister, Roslyn, left the next day. Within twenty-four hours of arriving at Mayo Clinic in Minnesota, she finally got a diagnosis of pancreatic cancer.

At the end of April, she came home, and was immediately placed in the hospice house, straight from the plane. The doctor there ordered a pain pump. We first thought she went there for pain management, but she continued to go downhill.

Now we knew my mom was terminally ill, but I didn't get a chance to talk to her because this came up so suddenly. My mother was in denial, not about the disease, but she didn't have time to process the fact that she was dying. She had a little bit of hope that she could seek treatment, but hospice said, "No, this is terminal." She was in shock and said she didn't want to die. I said, "I don't want you to die either!" It was so hard. The social worker asked her if she had a pre-planned funeral. She answered, "I thought I was here for pain management!"

The first night after she came back from Mayo, she sent the family home, saying she'd be fine there by herself. She refused when I offered to stay there with her. I went home, packed a bag, and drove back to the hospice house.

When I returned, she said, "I'm so glad you came back!" I said, "Mom, I wouldn't leave you alone."

She cried, and was happy I came back. They say they don't want you there, but they do. I'm the baby, and have two living siblings, but I'm hands-on and wanted to be there for her. In the mornings, I went home, made a meal, went to work, and then back to Mom every night for the overnight shift.

My mom was sometimes unconscious and couldn't tell me if she had pain. The nurses said to look for a frown or tensed up muscles. My sister and brother took turns during the day, so she was never alone. She came in and out a bit here and there, said a couple things, and went back to sleep. The medications were so strong, but you don't have a choice.

I relied on my faith in God during that time. I'm thankful I had the assurance of my mom's strong faith too. She practiced her faith every day of her life. My mom was brought up that way, and the real evidence was her giving, loving, and kind heart, every day. She never judged people and was so lovely and Christlike. Although she was human, I look at her life and say, "Wow!" I think sometimes when we're brought up in the faith, we don't totally grasp it until later in life. I know my mom's view got bigger as she aged. She was brought up with a narrow perspective. I would say she gained a greater knowledge of the grace of God in her latter years.

On Saturday, the nurses were saying she wouldn't make it through the night. I stayed there Saturday and Sunday and didn't leave. I learned so much about the dying process. My daughter stayed overnight with me at the hospice house so I wouldn't be alone. I was running on this weird adrenaline. The hardest part for me was seeing her go through the struggle. To me, it's comparable to the birth of a child. That struggle, dying, is hard work! The body doesn't want to give it up. The spirit wants to go. The body was built for survival. That's the way God created it. It doesn't shut down easily. The blood will come to the core of the body. Labored breathing is such hard work. I hope and pray she was not conscious enough to feel the pain and struggle at the end. My daughter woke me at 5 a.m., to tell me to come to her side, because my mom was taking her last breaths. She died only ten days after coming home from Mayo Clinic. So much had happened in only six months.

The funeral visitations keep you so busy. I suddenly stepped into the role of being responsible for the decisions and did all the planning. We didn't have time to make decisions together, so I wasn't sure what my mom wanted. We had visitation one night at their church, Harlem Reformed. My parents both attended their whole lives and married there, so everyone knew them. The funeral home kept her body overnight in the fellowship hall. The next day the funeral was also there.

Here's a cute one about my mom. She said we could see her in the casket, and a few close friends, but she didn't want others looking at her during funeral visitation. We had a private viewing of her body early, and invited a few people. It required a lot of phone calls to inform some family and close friends about coming. I also had my own special time alone with her. Then we had the casket closed. Once they close it, the funeral attendants say they will not open it again, out of respect to the person who passed away.

My mom had never taken a pill until she got sick with cancer. She was such a vibrant person, in phenomenal health until her last few months. Right up until she became sick, she was giving out food from the trucks in the church parking lot. My parents drove out to Texas, to spend winters there until their last years. Some people think, "Oh, they were eighty-one." But if you knew what they could still do!

It was a funeral; it wasn't called a celebration. We included some positive aspects to it, but it was sad! I'm kind of a real person, and for me to put on a happy face and say, "Woo-hoo!" isn't my style. It was a great loss. I wanted to talk about the hope we have, but grieve this very special person. I think you need to feel this, or you don't heal. Some people think if you're a Christian, you don't grieve. You very much do! You go through the exact same process. I tried to escape grief when my brother died, and it tackled me later.

For me, it's not like I can say, "They're in heaven, everything's beautiful." You can't just push it aside. Sooner or later you're going to have to go through the grief. The first time you go through the grieving process you don't know what to expect. Sometimes you think, *Am I going crazy?*

When someone close to you passes away, all the other recent deaths of loved ones flood back into your mind. I relived the actual moments of their deaths. I would continually go back to them because of watching them go through great suffering. After that first year, it gets better. I watched my mom go from being healthy and energetic to basically skeletal within a short period. It was really sad.

Since I work with elderly people cleaning homes or taking them to appointments, I had committed to these dear people, and didn't want to say, "Sorry I can't come to help you, I'm grieving." I couldn't say a prayer to make the grief disappear. There was a lot of crying and praying, but I got up every day and did what I had to do. Sometimes you feel like you're going to die. There's not an easy fix because we're human.

Late at night when all my family is in bed, sometimes I allow myself to grieve. Grief comes in waves. During the day I'm busy, but it often comes at night. You go under the wave. You sob and sob, wondering if it's ever going to end, but it does. You go through guilt, but people need to know that much of the guilt you carry is irrational. A friend had to tell me once, "Hope, that's not even true. There was nothing you could do about it; you pile guilt on yourself."

I'm strange about letting anyone become like a mentor to me. I had the best of the best for a mom, and I'm not willing to let anyone go there. Although I love my elderly friends, I don't have that kind of maternal bond with anyone else and keep a boundary. I know my mom's in heaven, and I want to keep my memories I have left. I don't want new feelings overriding the memories I have about my mom. My friends are all very kind, but I feel she's irreplaceable. I guess you remember your mom for what she did and who she was. She was such a great mom who took care of all of us, and was a devoted wife. She had a lot of close girlfriends because people really trusted her. They brought their cares and worries because she had very big shoulders and listened to them. At the funeral, the pastor said, "All these women kept coming up to me, saying, Arlene was their best friend. I thought, *You're going to have to duke it out!*"

While your parents are here, you just enjoy them. Later you take the time to reflect on who they were. You realize how important love is. She was such a genuine person because of her relationship with God. My mom taught me how to love—how to love right, and how important love is. My parents' love was beautiful. I'm thankful for my mother's wedding rings and her twenty-fifth anniversary ring, and never take them off. It reminds me of them.

When you're younger, you think you won't model after your mother, but you do. Before they're gone, they might irritate you, and when they die you feel like they were perfect. That's okay; they should get respect. Now and then I hear her in my own voice. I'll be talking to my kids, and I'll think I sound like my mom. Or I'll glace at my hands and think they look like my mom's.

My mom's death affected my kids, especially my daughter. She said, "She's not going to be at my wedding." Boys are a little different, but I believe they grieve in their own way. We bring them up to be strong.

My mom and I had open communication with each other. As I got older, we could talk about anything. She confided in me, and she was like a true best friend, yet she was my mom. It was a much deeper relationship. You'll do anything when trying to help your mom. I was only able to do all that for her by God's grace. It's just day by day, God gives the ability to do what is necessary.

The only way I can explain it is that my greatest hope is in the Lord, and my hope comes from Him. I can't understand how people go through this without hope. Without hope, there's nothing.

I don't think anyone passes through grief without changing somewhat. It does change who you are. I hope it changed me in a good way. Now I can't call my mom to discuss things, I have to step up to the plate. It's necessary to go directly to the Father or to the Word. I'm sure I have grown in my faith, and qualities like compassion.

When you experience the death of a close loved one, you realize how sad it really is. Now I pick up the phone more to listen to friends. At the funeral home, it hasn't even hit you yet. We need support later, after things have calmed down. Other people have lives and they move on. Your heart is just lying out there, broken. It has really opened my eyes to see this in others. They need a friend.

You're closer to your mom than you think you are, after she has passed away. As long as you're breathing, there's still a part of her that's always going to be alive. That's what's so beautiful about it. You were created from her. At first, I felt panic because I would never see her again. But if you really sit and think, and look deep inside yourself, maybe not in the physical sense, but you can still feel her. I still feel my mom. It's deeper and richer. I've gotten to the point now that I don't dread that I miss her. What a gift I was given to have someone so wonderful in my life. Not everyone gets that.

When you go through the grieving process, you feel like an important part of you is severed. Later, you realize there is a part of them you'll always have, so close to your heart. You feel like you're not going to survive it, but the love line is never completely severed. It transcends all. Love endures forever. Although you can't experience her face-to-face now, you experience her in your heart. I know I will see her again in heaven.

I discovered I haven't talked to anyone this in-depth about my mom's death. People ask, "How ya doin'?" They don't take the time to hear the whole thing. You don't really want to be negative and tell them all of it either. Most times it remains surface talk. I attended a couple of grief sessions at hospice. I've learned you have to give yourself a huge amount of grace for a very long time. When you have a broken leg, people see that. But when you're broken on the inside with grief, you have to deal with it and talk about it.

Bible verse and song:

My parents were gospel quartet fans. Most of the songs are based on scripture passages. One of the songs, by the Gaithers, speaks about Jesus's blood that gives strength from day to day, never loses its power, and reaches to the deepest valley. *(The Blood Will Never Lose Its Power)*

*Three things will last forever— faith, hope and love—and the greatest of these is love.* 1 Corinthians 13:13 NLT

"Love endures forever" is meaningful to me, and that's what I had engraved on my parents' gravestone. It's a promise from God's Word.

# Chapter 36

## A Very Long Goodbye

## With Judy Dunagan

*Judy was fifty-six at the time of the interview. Her mom, Anita, was eighty-four when she died on January 8, 2013, when Judy was fifty-three.*

My mother was seventy years old when she was first diagnosed with Alzheimer's. She battled the disease for fourteen years, while my father faithfully cared for her in their home in Phoenix for most of those years. Many who have loved ones battling Alzheimer's, refer to the disease as the "long goodbye," as they slowly fade away from us.

I will never forget when I found a note my mother had written before Alzheimer's stole her beautiful handwriting. On a yellow sticky note, she had written, "I'm fading away, but Jesus is keeping me every day." At the bottom of that note she wrote, "Hebrews 12:1–2," which in many ways defined her life.

The day before my mom died, my dad called to let me know the Lord was taking her home soon. She was dying from complications from her disease. Dad stayed by her side. I could hear her labored breathing in the background, as he talked to me. Later that night, a dream woke me, and I was troubled and crying. It seemed the Holy Spirit was prompting me to look at the clock. It was 2:30 a.m., and I wondered if my mom was perhaps going to heaven around that time. I put some worship music on to try to fall back asleep. Later that morning, on January 8, the phone rang around 4:30 a.m. Dad called to tell me Mom had passed away. Her caretaker later confirmed she died between 2:30 and 3:00 a.m. It's really sweet that I was awake and listening to worship music when she was on her way to Glory.

Thankfully, the morning of her death, I was able to book a flight to leave that same morning. So, by one o'clock that afternoon, Phoenix time, I was walking into my dad's home. I was able to relieve my exhausted dad and tell him to go rest while we handled things. Neighbors and friends stopped by, which was thoughtful but so tiring for him. I'm a do-er, so it was good to be able to help my dad on the first day. You don't realize how much there is to do. We were in planning mode, so you don't process the emotional side of it. My mom did quite a bit of early planning for her funeral, so that took stress off her daughters and husband. Mom and Dad had picked out the burial plot and casket. We were glad they did some preplanning, as it assured us that my parents' wishes were honored.

While my mom was in the midst of chemo for Hodgkin's disease, she was also diagnosed with Alzheimer's. She got through the Hodgkin's, but the Alzheimer's kept progressing. She had incredible strength. Alzheimer's is different than a sudden death or accident. We were longing for the Lord to take her home toward the end, for her to be out of her suffering and with her Savior. But we still missed her presence in our midst.

My mom had a very deep faith that was evident even while dealing with the trauma of Alzheimer's taking her sharp mind away. In her childlike way, she often shared Christ with strangers in grocery stores or restaurants. She had the gift of evangelism and shared Christ boldly with others. In her Bible, I found after she passed away, she had underlined scriptures and wrote "Praise the Lord" in her own way even when she no longer could spell words like "praise" and "Lord." Toward the end, when she could no longer carry on a conversation, she could still sing hymns with my dad. It showed her depth of faith.

My two daughters don't have any memory of my mom without Alzheimer's because they were young when she was diagnosed. I think Alzheimer's affected them more than my mother's death itself. One of my daughters was in medical school and couldn't come back for the funeral. She took up the challenge to write a tribute to her grandmother, and it was profound. I struggled with my mom's illness, wrestling with God about it, thinking, *Why should she have to struggle so long and lose her mind to this disease?* And I often wondered how it affected my daughters. But I know they will never forget the love story of their grandparents. My dad showed his bride so much dignity and honor. He never acted embarrassed about things she did. Their "until death do us part" lifelong commitment will impact generations to come. My daughters will also never forget my mother's deep faith in the midst of her suffering.

My daughter wrote, "If my grandma knew the impact having Alzheimer's would have on her family, she would have signed up for it." I think the impact it had in our family was greater than it would have been without it. It's the mystery of the gospel, how your greatest pain can have the greatest impact on others for eternity.

I'm incredibly blessed with a wonderful mother-in-law, now eighty-four, who is very sharp. She's been such a wonderful grandmother to my girls. We loved having her at family occasions and at my daughters' weddings. Also, I have a prayer warrior/friend/mentor who is twenty years older who filled a gap. She's been a prayer warrior for my girls too. I met Joanne three or four years after my mom was diagnosed, and as my mom was fading away, she became like a surrogate mother to me. I encourage women to have a mentor. The younger woman sometimes has to seek it out to make it happen.

It would have been neat if my mom could have met my sons-in-law, as they are both answers to her prayers for godly husbands for our daughters. And I know she'd be so blessed to see how happy my husband and I are. It's a joyful season of life as grandchildren are expanding our family. I'm sure the Lord tells her, "She's doing great," but I wish I could pick up the phone to tell her these things sometimes.

After my mom was gone, her value became even more prominent than while she was here on earth. She brought so much to our family. I think it's a mother-daughter thing to get more annoyed with your mom, and your dad can walk on water. I want to live my life so I can leave that kind of legacy, so, as a mom, I try to occasionally ask my children if there's anything I should ask their forgiveness for. I'd like to get those things settled now. Think about your funeral and what your family would say. It's not about looking good, it's about leaving the kind of legacy you hope to leave.

She had a sanguine personality and sang much of the time. She loved keeping the house clean, and she was a joyful woman who loved having people in the home. The holidays were always so wonderful with delicious food and celebrations as a family. A sweet memory that keeps returning is my mom making dresses for my sisters and me for Easter. She was an artist in her sewing. She had beautiful taste in the fabric she chose. I miss her the most at Easter because she made it fun. Even though she was such a busy pastor's wife, we'd get new hats, we made Easter baskets, and we hid eggs around the house. It was her favorite time of the year because Jesus Christ's death and resurrection secure our eternity with Him and her hope for that was unwavering. Because of Christ's death and resurrection, I know I will see my mother again. I have the hope and assurance of Christ in me.

Someday I'd love to know more about Alzheimer's because it was hard to know how much she knew about what was happening around her. My dad prayed over her, that the Lord would meet her in the confusion of Alzheimer's as only He could do. I know He did, and I'd like to know what it was like for her.

I'd like to ask my mom if I might have hurt her. As daughters, I think there's some wounding that can happen with moms that you never talk about. I was blessed to have the mom that I did. But if a daughter had a rough time, or there was some wounding and it didn't get resolved between them, the enemy wants to twist that. I'm sure it's even harder if you lose your mom younger or if you have children after she dies. I can't imagine the pain. Seek out what you need while in your grief and don't try to just get over the loss quickly. Get counseling if needed! There shouldn't be any shame in that. Be in tune with your heart.

As women, we need to understand the depth of the pain when our mothers die. No matter what age the daughter is when her mom passes away, she is somewhat orphaned. After her passing, I began to process the beauty of who my mom was and her legacy even more.

Bible Verses:

*When I awake, I will see you face to face and be satisfied.* Psalm 17:15 NLT

This verse meant so much to me when my mother passed away, especially because before her death, she no longer recognized the faces of her family. I love to think that the first face she recognized after all those years was the face of Jesus. Perhaps when she first saw Him face-to-face, she even said, "Oh, it's You!"

*Therefore, since we have so great a cloud of witnesses surrounding us, let us also lay aside every encumbrance and the sin which so easily entangles us, and let us run with endurance the race that is set before us, fixing our eyes on Jesus, the author and perfecter of faith, who for the joy set before Him endured the cross, despising the shame, and has sat down at the right hand of the throne of God.* Hebrews 12:1-2 NASB

I found this reference on two sticky notes my mother had written before Alzheimer's stole her handwriting. I call that my sticky note legacy and these verses have become my life verses.

# RESOURCES

## Healing Balm for The Soul

1. Get together for lunch near Mother's Day with friends who have lost their mothers. Each person brings a memento or memory to share. Give each person a turn with undivided attention. Celebrate those mothers who have gone before.
2. Pray.
3. Exercise.
4. Seek out fellowship and support in your church.
5. Talk with friends.
6. Create a photo album of your mom.
7. Take prayer walks.
8. Write/journal/blog.
9. Write a book about your mom.
10. Play music she liked, or you enjoyed together.
11. Make up a bucket list.
12. Light a candle at meaningful times.
13. Make a cookbook of your mom's favorite recipes.
14. Donate your time to elderly or infant care.
15. Sponsor a child from World Vision in your mom's honor.
16. Make a quilt out of mom's shirts.
17. Construct a shadow box of your mom's most precious items.

18. Take long baths.
19. Allow, or even schedule grieving time, to cry, or talk with God about your mom.
20. Place flowers on Mom's grave.
21. Reminisce with family members.
22. Attend a meeting for Grief Share, or a similar program.
23. Get Christian counseling.
24. Do something special on birthdays and death dates, like donating to a charity.
25. Practice taking good care of yourself.
26. Breathing exercises—deep breathing.
27. Write notes in balloons and let them go.
28. Plant a tree in honor of your mom.
29. Spend periods of time in nature.
30. Choose a charity for a memorial fund.
31. Write a letter to yourself from your mom's perspective—what she'd tell you.
32. Display photos in special frames.
33. Read a book on grief.
34. Honor another mother on Mother's Day.
35. Buy a Christmas ornament each year in honor of your mom.
36. The family writes favorite memories, or her sayings; place them in a Christmas stocking.
37. Participate in a healing prayer session with believers.
38. Attend your local hospice bereavement meetings.
39. Write out/search for favorite mom quotes/poems.
40. Read the Bible.
41. Spend an afternoon on the beach or on a mountain.
42. Have a piece of Mom's jewelry made into a special necklace or ring.
43. Write a letter to God.
44. Mentor a younger woman.
45. Seek out an older woman to be your mentor.
46. Take time to be still and rest in God's presence.

Myrna Folkert

# Bible Verses to Comfort and Encourage

*God is our refuge and strength, an ever-present help in trouble.* Psalm 46:1

*Those who hope in the LORD will renew their strength. They will soar on wings like eagles; they will run and not grow weary; they will walk and not be faint.* Isaiah 40:31

*Come to me, all you who are weary and burdened, and I will give you rest. Take my yoke upon you and learn from me, for I am gentle and humble in heart, and you will find rest for your souls. For my yoke is easy and my burden is light.* Matthew 11:28–30

*Wait for the LORD; be strong and take heart and wait for the LORD.* Psalm 27:14

*We are hard pressed on every side, but not crushed; perplexed, but not in despair; persecuted, but not abandoned; struck down, but not destroyed.* 2 Corinthians 4:8–9

*Praise be to the God and Father of our Lord Jesus Christ, the Father of compassion and the God of all comfort, who comforts us in all our troubles, so that we can comfort those in any trouble with the comfort we ourselves receive from God. For just as we share abundantly in the sufferings of Christ, so also our comfort abounds through Christ. If we are distressed, it is for your comfort and salvation; if we are comforted, it is for your comfort which produces in you patient endurance of the same sufferings we suffer. And our hope for you is firm, because we know that just as you share in our sufferings, so also you share in our comfort.* 2 Corinthians 1:3–7

*So, do not fear, for I am with you; do not be dismayed, for I am your God. I will strengthen you and help you; I will uphold you with my righteous right hand.* Isaiah 41:10

*My Father's house has many rooms; if that were not so, would I have told you that I am going there to prepare a place for you? And if I go and prepare a place for you, I will come back and take you to be with me that you also may be where I am.* John 14:2–3

*I saw the Holy City, the new Jerusalem, prepared as a bride beautifully dressed for her husband. And I heard a loud voice from the throne . . . He will wipe every tear from their eyes. There will be no more death or mourning or crying or pain, for the old order of things has passed away. . . To the thirsty I will give water without cost from the spring of the water of life. Those who are victorious will inherit all this, and I will be their God and they will be my children. . .The Holy City . . . shone with the glory of God, and its brilliance was like that of a very precious jewel, like a jasper, clear as crystal. . . The wall was made of jasper, and the city of pure gold, as pure as glass. The foundations of the city walls were decorated with every kind of precious stone. . .each gate made of a single pearl. . . The great street of the city was of gold, as pure as transparent glass. . . The city does not need the sun or the moon to shine on it, for the glory of God gives it light . . . there will be no night there.* Revelation 21:2-25 (condensed by author)

*Not only so, but we also glory in our sufferings, because we know that suffering produces perseverance; perseverance, character; and character, hope. And hope does not put us to shame, because God's love has been poured out into our hearts through the Holy Spirit, who has been given to us.* Romans 5:3–5

*May the God of hope fill you with all joy and peace as you trust in him, so that you may overflow with hope by the power of the Holy Spirit.* Romans 15:13

# Support and Helps

**Songs**

Handel's Messiah, by George Frideric Handel and Charles Jennens (in Mary's story)

"The Hallelujah Chorus" from Handel's Messiah, by George Frideric Handel, and Charles Jennens (in Jodi's story)

"I Can Only Imagine," by MercyMe ( in Rachael S.'s story)

"In Christ Alone," by Kristian Stanfill (in Kari's story)

"Blessed be the Name of the Lord," by Matt Redman (in Carla's and Julie's stories)

"How Great Thou Art," by Carl Boberg (in Marie's, Julie's, and Rachel B.'s stories)

"How Firm a Foundation," by John Rippon (in Marie's story)

"Great Is Thy Faithfulness," by Thomas Chisholm and William Runyan (in Carla's and Marcia's stories)

"The Blood Will Never Lose Its Power," by Bill and Gloria Gaither (in Hope's story)

"It Is Well with My Soul," by Horatio G. Spafford (in Ruthann's and Joy's stories)

"Have Thine Own Way, Lord," by Adelaide A. Pollard (in Faith's story)

"Be Still My Soul," by Kathrina von Schlegel

"Even If," by MercyMe

**Organizations**

Living Threads, at City on a Hill, Zeeland, MI (quilts—in Kari's story)

Grief Share, a national organization for dealing with grief (in Nancy's story)

"Motherless Daughters," national and local meetings

Comfort Zone Camps—for children who have lost a loved one

Starlight Ministries, in Hudsonville, Michigan—work with teenagers who have lost a loved one

Various national, state, and private hospice care organizations

**Prayers**

Conception to Birth Prayer, (Back to the Womb prayers) Francis and Judith MacNutt School of Healing Prayer, Level I, facilitator's Manual, pages 153-165 (in Mary's story)

**Gifts**

Thummies: Thumbprint gifts can be found online, or some funeral homes will make them for you (in Rachel B's story)

Quilts—made from shirts or clothing of the deceased (in Kari's story)

**Books**

*Good Grief: 50th Anniversary Edition*, by Granger E. Westberg

*Living when a Loved One Has Died*, by Earl A. Grollman (in Judy B.'s story)

*A Grace Disguised*, by Jerry Sitzer (in Rachael S.'s story)

*Thank You for This Thorn*, by Jodi Vande Noord, one of the interviewees. It is placed in the hospice house of Pella, Iowa

*A Grief Observed*, by C. S. Lewis

*In My Mother's Kitchen*, by Robin A. Edgar

*It's OK That You're Not OK*, by Megan Devine

*Psalms of Lament*, by Ann Weems

## Sources/Research of Motherless Daughters

Comfort Zone Camps – Camps offered for children and teens who have lost a parent, guardian, or sibling. https://www.comfortzonecamp.org/

Comfort Zone Camps, research done by New York Life – polling research http://www.hellogrief.org/wp-content/uploads/2010/03/CZC-White-Paper-Grief-Research.pdf

Blog by Lisa Bonchek Adams and a book her family compiled, "Persevere: A Life with Cancer." https://lisabadams.com/2011/05/25/when-daughtersgrieve-the-death-of-their-mothers/https://www.amazon.com/Persevere-Cancer-Lisa-BonchekAdams/dp/099916290X

Article by Sandy Banks – Newspaper journalist tells about her mother loss. https://www.latimes.com/local/la-me-banks-motherless-daughters-20140503-column.html

Therapist Irene Rubaum-Keller – Keller's mother-loss story and formation of Motherless Daughter programs in the nation. https://www.huffpost.com/entry/we-never-get-overit_n_47866

# Discussion Questions

1. Have you lost someone close to you? Has your mother died? If so, how long ago was it, and how did it happen?
2. How was the topic of death dealt with in your family? Ignored? Taboo? Discussed openly?
3. How do you express your grief?
4. My greatest sense of loss has been...
5. What I fear the most about loss...
6. What is your most vivid image associated with the loss of your mom?
7. Do you have unhappy memories about your mom, or the circumstances surrounding her death?
8. What is the best memory you have about your mom?
9. Which woman's story can you relate to the most? Why? Talk about how your story correlates with hers.
10. Have you been affected by your mom's death in a negative way? What is something you regret concerning your mom?
11. Has anything concerning your mom's death ultimately affected you in a positive way?
12. What is something you're very happy you did or said?
13. Have you ever experienced delayed grief? What happened and was there a trigger?
14. If you went to counseling, was that a helpful experience?
15. What do you think you learned from your mom's death?
16. What could you teach another woman going through her mom's death?
17. Have you been mentored, or mentored someone else during grief?
18. What could someone do to help another along in their walk through grief and loss?
19. What is your greatest hope?
20. How has your faith helped you through deaths you've experienced?

21. What ways have you honored or celebrated your mom? Do you have additional ways of doing this besides the ones listed in this book?
22. In what ways do you think you have grown the most as a result of this loss?
23. What are some good books you'd recommend on death and grief?
24. What Bible verses do you know that are comforting during a loss?

# Get to Know the Daughters

The women who interviewed for this book shared their deeply personal stories for the purpose of giving hope to others who have lost their mothers. They bravely participated in order to encourage and give comfort to the readers. (Corresponding chapter numbers in parentheses)

**Marie Getz (10)** loves biking, hiking, or most anything out in God's beautiful world, catching every sunrise and sunset possible. These activities, plus extensive journaling, have been helpful in bringing peace and clarity of mind to her journey through daily life. She's married to her husband Seth; they have three children, Christian, Claire, and Aerianna, and their fur-baby Rocky, living in Holland, Michigan.

**Mary Sterenberg (11)** is an ordained pastor in the Christian Reformed Church. She worked as a Registered Occupational Therapist as a business consultant. Mary held positions in her denomination as a prayer mobilizer and prayer coordinator. She has served in Presbyterian Reformed Ministries International (PRMI) on the Board of Directors, and as a teacher of prayer at Dunamis Institute throughout North America. She was the co-chair for the Grand Rapids CityFest Prayer Team for the Luis Palau Association in 2018. Mary serves as the pastor of prayer and spirituality at Discovery Christian Reformed Church in West Michigan. She is married to Bruce. They have three married children, their spouses, and seven grandchildren. Mary is a painter, inspired by the revelation of God in nature. She is the creator of

*Hermina (Buni) Morren, holding Mary*

her business, Sweet Mary's Bath and Body products, inventor of bath products and children's hand-sewn clothing. Her products are meant to share love and pampering with girls and women, who are created special and worthy by their Creator. See videos on prayer training here: https://vimeo.com/showcase/4431343

**Rebecca Deng (12)** is an international speaker with the American Bible Society Mission Trauma Healing program. She advocates for women and children who are victimized or traumatized by war. She has firsthand knowledge, as she was a refugee from South Sudan's Dinka Tribe. After escaping from her village as a very young child, she lost most of her family, and lived in a refugee camp for years, before coming to the United States in the year 2000. She was one of the eighty-nine Lost Girls who came to the United States around the same time as the Lost Boys of Sudan. Rebecca now lives in Holland, Michigan, married to her husband Jordan Roeda, with three children, Cholie, Deng Jakob, and Leona. Rebecca tells her complete story in her book, which was released in the fall of 2019. More information available here: *What They Meant for Evil: How a Lost Girl of Sudan Found Healing, Peace, and Purpose in the Midst of Suffering.* Go to rebeccadeng.com for more information.

**Carla (13)** has been married to an amazing man for nine years, and together they have been blessed with two children, a girl and a boy. She loves helping out in the nursery and as a leader and teacher in her church. Inspired by her mom, who was a nurse, Carla is a nurse in the birth center of a local hospital. She also claims the labels of daughter, sister, and friend. Above all, Carla knows her identity as a child of God and desires to forever praise and glorify Him for His love and faithfulness to her.

**Lisa (14)** graduated from college with a teaching degree but didn't become a teacher. God's plan and timing for that degree have become clear now, since she is presently the Children's Ministry Coordinator at her church, dedicating time and energy to help kids grow in their relationship with Christ. Lisa has been married to her fabulous husband for thirteen years. They have a daughter and a son. They love to spend time outdoors, especially in the summer, soaking up the Michigan sunshine.

**Marilyn Tinklenberg (15)** is a dedicated wife to her preacher husband, Duane, mother to three, grandmother to eleven, and great-grandmother to thirteen. They attend as many sporting, music, theatre, and concert events for their grands as they can. If that doesn't keep her busy enough, Marilyn does alterations and sewing for many people. In her free time, she loves to read, do counted cross stitch, and crocheting. She attended Reformed Bible Institute in Grand Rapids, Michigan, which is now called Kuyper College, for a short time before having her children. Because of the ministry, they have lived in various towns in the Midwest, but now can be found in Sioux Center, Iowa.

*Tena Vander Woude, holding Marilyn, 1943*

**Carol Teske (16)** is married to her husband, Clay, who is a U.S. Air Force retiree, and they have one daughter. They have lived in many different states, and in Germany for four years. She worked as a registered nurse for thirty years, loves to be out in nature, and has a passion for animals. The pet therapy visits she did with her Golden Retriever to hospitals and mental health facilities over the years, were the most rewarding of any volunteer activities she has done. Carol is thankful she began with a solid foundation, to be born into a loving, God-fearing family. She enjoys gardening flowers and ornamentals, playing piano for relaxation, and has worked with Habitat for Humanity.

*Tena Vander Woude, holding Carol, 1945*

**Nancy Maas (17)** is a retired elementary and special services teacher who still enjoys teaching a MOPS preschool class, as well as Children and Worship at her church. After nearly forty years of marriage, she lost her husband, Wally, to Lewy body dementia in 2012, which eventually led her to become a Grief Share facilitator. Her family consists of three married children and their spouses, three grandsons, and four granddaughters. Her hobbies and interests are gardening, reading,

*Bertha Vander Woude, holding Nancy, with sisters, Marilyn and Carol, 1949*

singing, Bible study, hiking, and spending quality time with family and friends—especially her grandchildren! She recently married Dave Visser, and they make their home in the beautiful state of Washington.

**Faith VanArendonk (18)** and her husband reside in the great plains of South-Central Iowa. They have been blessed with two children, their spouses, and eight grandchildren. She enjoys spending time with her family, as well as volunteering at her church, and her grandchildren's school. Faith's interests include working on the yard, walking, reading, and socializing with friends.

*Faith with mom, Bertha Vander Woude holding sister Joanne, 1954*

**Kari (19)** is married to her incredible, loving husband, and they have two sweet and spunky boys. Her heart is filled with love for the three of them and for God. Kari graduated from Grand Valley State University, and is a sales manager at an athletic club. She and her family love to hike, travel, and make adventures out of everyday life, because if there's one thing she learned since her mom passed away, it is that each day we are blessed with is truly a gift.

**Elaine Stock (20)** is an award-winning author of women's and inspirational fiction to uplift with hopes of better tomorrows. Her novel, *Her Good Girl*, is a three-time winner of "Outstanding" Christian Fiction. Born in Brooklyn, New York, Elaine has now been living in upstate, rural New York with her husband for more years than her stint as a NYC gal. She enjoys long walks down country roads, visiting New England towns, and of course, a good book. You can visit her website at https://www.elainestock.com

**Karen Blakley (21)** lives a very busy life as a mother to three adult children, and a grandmother to five. She still works part-time as a registered nurse, and fulfills many volunteer positions and missionary opportunities. She wears many hats at her church, for the Holland Rescue Mission, Bible Study Fellowship leader, and Bibles for Mexico Leadership committee. Karen continues to make mission trips with Living Water International, which drills wells in impoverished countries, teaching hygiene, and teaching about Christ, the true Living Water. She also makes mission trips to Guatemala, through Grace ministries. If all that doesn't keep her busy enough, she loves to work in her flower garden, and is a book club member.

*Karen at age two, with her mom, Mary*

**Rachael Smith (22)** was challenged by her mother, from a young age, to always remain calm, cool, and collected. She thinks she has yet to accomplish this, because of her daily chaos, which includes being a wife, a mom to three, and the director of a nonprofit, called, *Oh Lord Help Us*, which supports women, especially those aging out of foster care. Rachael attempts to keep her sanity by running, and staying close to Jesus. She and her family call Rolesville, North Carolina their home. You can find her on the website https://www.ohlordhelp.us, to see what all the excitement is about.

**Vanessa Jorge (23)** is a born and raised Jersey Girl, with a strong Latino upbringing. Her mother instilled in her the importance of self-awareness and transformation. Vanessa often tips a glass of wine in honor of her mom, especially on the anniversary of her death each year, because her mom was somewhat of a wine connoisseur. Currently working as a civil engineer, she makes time for family and friends, going to the gym, and volunteering at the local animal shelter. She would do a happy dance if you looked up her blog at http://civil-seeker.tumblr.com/ where she writes stories about the honest pain of her mom's death, and living a life of discovery and healthier habits.

*Vanessa with her mom, Laura, 2004*

**Ruthann David (24)** has a servant's heart and uses it everywhere. Since she is a retired special educator, she is equipped to work as a Kids Hope mentor, works in the children's program for Celebrate Recovery, and is a Sunday school teacher for special needs adults. She likes to tell the story of getting married for the first time, at age fifty-three, to her hubby Ray, whom she had dated as a young lady. They've now celebrated their twenty-second anniversary. She has eleven step grandchildren through her husband, which keeps her running. Ruthann loves to cook, read, sew, and knit, if there's ever any leftover time.

*Ruthann with her mom, Doris, 1945*

**Judy Boeve (25)** is a paraprofessional at an elementary school, assisting students in working to their potential in reading and math. She's a wife, mom to a son, a married daughter, and her son-in-law. Well known for her cooking and baking skills, she loves to grace others when she can, with a hot dish or a plate of goodies. She carves out time to do a little sewing, scrapbooking, and gardening in her little town of Hamilton, Michigan. Judy is a prayer warrior who has a huge heart for anyone in need.

*Judy, age three, with mom, Angeline, Kollen Park, Holland, MI*

**Rachel Brink (26)** resides in West Michigan, with her wonderful husband of twelve years. They have two pups, Penny, and Pete, who think they are humans, entertaining and keeping them busy. Rachel loves to run, play tennis, and spend time with family and friends. After completing grad school, she worked at Love INC, (In the Name of Christ) a nonprofit which assists those in need in the community, as a social worker. Now, taking a break for other endeavors, she runs her own business out of her home, cooking and baking for Brinks Bakery Shoppe. Rachel also works for her "adopted" family at the Holland Peanut Store. She loves to encourage and help others everywhere she goes. https://www.facebook.com/BrinksBakeryShoppe

*Rachel with mom, Karen, 2006*

**Janice Broyles (27)** holds a doctorate in Educational Leadership, and teaches at Living Stone College. She is the third of four children and grew up in a loving home with parents who worked hard to provide. She is now married, has two sons and a dog, and lives in North Carolina. She enjoys writing fiction and non-fiction, and sharing Jesus with those around her. Check out Janice's website at www.janicebroyles.com, to see what she's up to or to purchase her books.

**Michele Dekker (28)** takes great joy in her two adult sons, Michael and Jeffrey. Jeffrey is married to Katelin. Michele loves to gather both of her young grandsons, Cole, and Grant, on her lap to read a stack of children's books. Michele has been a registered nurse for thirty-seven years and cares for people at an ophthalmology center in Holland, Michigan. She loves to garden, read, spend time with family and friends, and still finds time to volunteer at her local church. Michele enjoys traveling, and recently returned from a trip to the Holy Land.

**Joy Meyer (29)** has been happily married to her hog farmer husband for thirty-five years. They have five adult children, two sons, and three daughters, and now have added two daughters-in-law, and one son-in-law. Her two grandsons, and three granddaughters keep her on her toes nowadays. You might find Joy in the farmyard, helping out with the chores, reading, or in her kitchen, cooking and baking, with one of those little ones on her hip. Joy never tires of the beauty of sunrises and sunsets in the farm country they call their home, in Drenthe, Michigan.

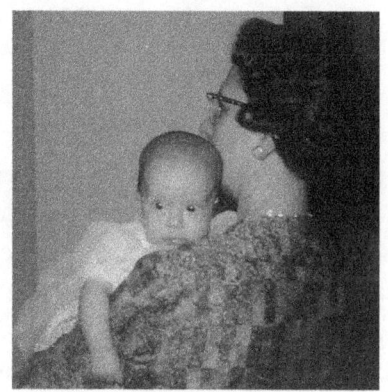

*Joy and Mom, Ruth, baptism, 1964*

**Pat Lubben (30)** and her husband have learned to ballroom dance. Traveling to interesting places is frequently near the top of her list. Pat enjoys hiking out in God's beautiful world, discovering mountains, lakes, animals, and sunsets. Besides all these pastimes, Pat is an educator, and the mother of three adult children and their families, which makes her a grandmother of one.

**Julie Peters (31)** takes joy in being married to her best friend, Mike, for twenty-four years. She's been a stay-at-home mom to their six children, between the ages of eleven and twenty-one. Julie took on the job of homeschooling each of their kids for around five of their school years. She earned a bachelor's degree in health science at Grand Valley State University, and now works in the fitness industry part-time. Julie has volunteered at church in various ways as a teacher and mentor. She and her husband have been youth group leaders, and marriage mentors. As a family, they enjoy spending time together outdoors, camping, or hiking. Julie has always fondly called the little town of Hamilton, Michigan, her home, where the cornfields wave in the summer breezes.

**Jodi Vande Noord (32)** is a wife, and mom of teenagers, living among the midwestern farmlands. Daily transporting and attending her teens' activities keeps her busy. Jodi meets interesting people each day on the job at a counseling center. She loves outdoor activities, gardening, exercising, sporting events, and raising pets. Besides managing her household and job, in all her free time, Jodi can be found writing stories and articles. Jodi also wrote a book, called *Thank You for This Thorn*, about her mother-loss, which is

*Sandi Heinen with Jodi, age six, 1980*

kept at the hospice house in Pella, Iowa, for visitors to read. Check out her blog and follow her, at https://www.jodimnoord.com

**Prudy Berghorst (33)** and her husband, Jon, have five children and twelve grandchildren who keep them busy. They do the live-in babysitting gig whenever possible, which brings them across the country to their grandchildren. She attended Muskegon Community College, and Spring Arbor College, with a Registered Nursing Degree. She used her skills in various hospitals and clinics, and as a missionary in Russia for two years. In her retirement, she enjoys creating beautiful quilts, and collecting china sets. Prudy takes strides to be an available, prayerful friend in her family, church, and community.

**Marcia (34)** is a former pediatric nurse who uses her caring nature to work as a volunteer at a nonprofit organization, called Love INC, (In the Name of Christ) which shares the love of Christ by mentoring and assisting those in need in her community. She supports her hog farmer husband, in West Michigan. The mother of two married children and their spouses, Marcia loves to spend time with her six grandchildren. She often curls up with a good book, is active in her church, and frequently uses her marvelous cooking skills to bring cheer to others.

**Hope Doolaard (35)** has a soft heart for the elderly, and has a side business working in their homes, cleaning, cooking, doing errands, or just alleviating their loneliness by taking the time to chat. She also likes to volunteer with the opposite end of the age spectrum, by teaching Children in Worship in her church, which utilizes a storytelling format and multisensory materials. Hope has been married for twenty-nine

*Hope with mom, Arlene, 1995*

years, and has two adult children. She is always on the spot for do-it-yourself projects, at home, or for others. You might find Hope baking a batch of cookies for her church or community friends, in Western Michigan.

**Judy Dunagan (36)** served as a women's ministry leader before joining Moody Publishers as an Acquisitions Editor for the women's line of books and other discipleship resources. She helped launch a new women's Bible study line at Moody, and loves equipping aspiring authors and speakers. A wonder seeker who chases knowledge of God and His Word, Judy is passionate about discipling women and making God's Word come alive in everyday life. Now she's enjoying an empty nest with her husband, Rick, in the Colorado Mountains, where she works remotely for Moody. They love being grandparents of Liam, Wim, and Quinn. Visit Judy's blog where she writes about legacy makers and wonder seekers at judydunagan.com

*Judy on her first day of school, with mom, Anita*

Myrna Folkert enjoys boating in West Michigan with her husband of thirty-six years. They have two adult sons. After teaching elementary school for twenty-seven years, she now volunteers for hospice, visiting patients, interviewing many about their lives. Myrna wrote devotionals for *Words of Hope*, and contributed to the anthology, *Christmas Presence*. Visit her website to read articles of memoir, and creative non-fiction, or to order her book, at www.myrnafolkert.com. You can also find her author page on Facebook, called, *Tablet of your Heart*.

Myrna Folkert

www.ingramcontent.com/pod-product-compliance
Lightning Source LLC
LaVergne TN
LVHW011153080426
835508LV00007B/371